C-SUITE

— AND —

BEYOND

THE 4 KEYS TO LEADERSHIP SUCCESS

TOM KERESZTI

RUTLEDGE
HILL

Published by HarperCollins Leadership, an imprint of HarperCollins Focus LLC.

Library of Congress Cataloging-in-Publication Data

Library of Congress Control Number: 2020917014

ISBN: 978-1-4002-2702-0 (TP)
ISBN: 978-1-4002-2701-3 (HC)
ISBN: 978-1-4002-2700-6 (E)

Printed in the United States of America.

Rutledge Hill rev. date: 09/08/2020

CONTENTS

INTRODUCTION

What is your road map to success? How do you know the road ahead when you have never been there yourself? In my Fortune 500 journey to the C suite and beyond, I've had many wins and failures as an executive and as a human being. By reflecting on and analyzing the times when I succeeded and the times when I failed, I was able to boil the reasons behind my successful achievements down to four key principles. I also noticed that successful leaders and successful companies share in following these same four principles. This gave me the inspiration for my new book, which discusses the four keys to leadership success. I believe that if you let these four keys guide your life, you will be led to success in your personal life and in business.

I wish that when I was a young manager someone would have given me a leadership road map like this. I thought I had all the answers, but it turned out that I needed a lot of guidance. I was fortunate to have worked for some brilliant business leaders and adopted some of their best practices. When I became a senior executive, I had to acquire a whole new leadership skill set, and I required even more know-how as an international executive. Each time, I observed the business leaders I looked up to and began to model myself after them. When I entered my next phase of maturity as a C-suite executive and a Christian leader, I underwent a transformation, including a paradigm shift in my leadership style. As I embark on the next phase of my life, I find it extremely rewarding to give back and share my experiences and what I've learned. I meet young executives through my workshops, and I take joy in coaching them to reach new heights. I love their energy, enthusiasm, and optimism and their hunger for growth. It is a blessing to guide them in the right direction and into the next phase of their careers as leaders.

Each phase of my career required additional skills, and a different set of skills, if I wanted to become successful. Whether you are an executive just starting out or one who is already well on your way, I would love to pass on some of the wisdom I've gained and to help you learn from my wins and losses. If you are entering the international arena as an expatriate leader, you will find many valuable lessons within these pages. And if you are trying to reconcile your faith with your workplace, you will enjoy *C Suite and Beyond* even more.

From 1992 to 2019 I lived and worked in six different countries and eight different cities, and as a result I attended a different church about every three years. One constant I noticed was that every church I attended always preached the same message: there is the evil secular business world, and the right way is defined only by the church. I never bought into that falsehood. Businesses can be, and in many instances are, led by Christian principles. In fact, I submit that if you take two similar businesses competing in the same market with identical products, with one of them following biblical principles and the other following secular principles, you will find that the one led by Christian principles will post higher sales and profits every time. Now there is no guarantee that a business led by a Christian will not be mismanaged, only a guarantee that successful businesses are probably already led by Christian principles, even if they are not aware of it. I assure you, the leadership principles outlined in *C Suite and Beyond* are all biblically based, although I omit the scriptural contexts except for in one chapter, so as not to alienate readers who do not share the same faith.

John Maxwell, who has written multiple *New York Times* best sellers, suggested that I should ask myself two questions before writing any book. The first question is, "Why should anyone want to read this book?" The second is, "How do I make the book interesting enough that the reader wants to turn the pages and continue reading?" There are many leadership experts who can only tell stories; they have never lived out those stories, so really they're only engaging in hearsay. I have lived out the stories I tell, and I would like to inspire you to reach new heights and add value to your life by sharing my experiences and what I've learned. As you read on, I hope you will be entertained by my lifetime collection of jolly stories. Along the way, I will also pass on some wisdom to help you become a better leader. At the end of each chapter, you will find a series of questions to help you reflect on your leadership journey. I encourage you to take some time and evaluate how you can grow as a leader.

If you are reading *C Suite and Beyond*, I suspect you're already a strong leader who realizes that you want to invest in yourself, continue improving, and reach new heights. So let's embark on this journey together to laugh at my stories and learn from my mistakes.

ACKNOWLEDGMENTS

This book would not be complete without acknowledgment of the people who touched my life and made me the person I have grown to become. I know it has not been easy for them to be by my side, but my family and friends helped me through adversity and also helped me celebrate my achievements.

My friend Shane, the brother I never had, who passed away too soon, taught me that hard work is meaningless unless you get to enjoy life along the way. Shane was the best man at my wedding and was godfather to my daughter Nicole. I met him in our freshman year of high school, and from that point on he was part of just about every chapter of my life. I remember having drinks a few years before he passed away. Shane raised his glass for a toast: "Thanks for the ride; it's been fun." That pretty much sums up our brotherhood.

My wife, Kathy, whom I met in 1976, has been the one stable reality check in my life. In her loving Irish and Italian way, she always keeps me humble and is the rock of our family. She has always supported me and shared in all my adventures, undoubtedly sacrificing some of her own dreams to do so. She has taught me that giving is a lot more fun than receiving. The best testimony of this that I can offer is our three adult daughters, who are flourishing in life. My girls Jen, Nikki, and Alex are the ones who keep me going each day. Their smiles, their hugs, and the lessons they have taught me about life through my parenting of them are more valuable than anything I could learn in a boardroom.

There is a saying: you can pick your friends but not your family. I have been blessed with my mom, grandmom, and sister, who spoil me and make me believe I am always the most important person on earth. I remember a line from the Michael J. Fox TV series *Spin City* where Caitlin, played by Heather Locklear, says: "Mike, believe it or not, the whole universe does not revolve around you." Michael J. Fox, playing Mike Flaherty, simply answers: "Are you calling my mom a liar?" That pretty much sums it up. I can do no wrong in my mom's eyes. Unconditional love is the most important value I learned from her. As a father, I love my kids unconditionally and support them with all that I have.

My Christian faith is the foundation of who I am. I thank Pastor Bob Zbiden for helping me realize I needed a paradigm shift to accept Christ and for baptizing me as an adult. Pastor Tim Anderson was a guiding force in my early journey after my adult baptism. Pastor Tom Mullins, who is an inspirational preacher, took my faith to new heights and helped me establish my Christ-centered life. And finally, thanks to John Maxwell, who helped me bridge my faith and my career and helped make me a better Christian leader.

In my corporate career spanning more than twenty-five years, I have come to admire three individuals and mentors whom I deeply respect. The first is Dr. Frank Morelli, from Colgate-Palmolive, who taught me about servant leadership and how to lead by example. The second is Bart Becht, CEO of Reckitt Benckiser, who taught me that marketing products is not rocket science, simply common sense with a knowledge of human behavior. The third is Erez Vigodman, CEO of the Strauss Group, who taught me to have a big appetite and a bold strategy for growth.

Well, that is the cast of main characters who helped shape my adult life, although you will read about many more colleagues and friends throughout *C Suite and Beyond*. So come along. Imagine you are in these stories, and chuckle as you ponder the life lessons.

1

LEADERSHIP IS INFLUENCE

I have met thousands of people in my life and have gotten to know hundreds of them. I can say that only a handful have influenced me to become the person I am. Some people influenced me on how to be a better husband, others on how to raise my kids, and still others on how to excel in business, and some showed me how to walk in faith. Influence happens in different ways; you will intentionally influence some people, while others will be passively influenced as they observe your behavior. In this chapter I will provide just a few examples of how people come to be influenced. It is my desire that as you read *C Suite and Beyond*, you learn through my experiences, and it is my hope that I will inspire you to be a better leader. I also hope that you not only lead people but also impact others positively so that they may learn to be a positive influence on others too.

All three of my daughters went through the terrible twos, you know, that age when kids begin to find their free will and start speaking out about what they want or do not want to do. Now, if you ask my kids, they will say I was always the softie pushover and Kathy was the discipliner. It takes a lot to get me rattled, but each of my girls pushed me too far at least once. The worst my soft style of discipline ever got was to enforce a time-out where the girls had to stand against a wall with their toes and noses touching it for a few minutes.

On two separate occasions with my older daughters, Jennifer and Nicole, I was able to influence their behavior as I'd intended. One time, I recall, I raised my voice and gave them a time-out. Both sobbing, they took the punishment and went to stand against the wall with their noses touching it. I tried this same approach with my youngest daughter, Alex, but she rebelled and simply refused. My influence had failed. This became clear when she turned to me and said, "Dad, you're crazy. I'm not doing that." No matter how much I insisted she do it and reminded her that I was her dad, she refused. She refused so many times that I finally burst out into laughter and gave up.

See, leadership does not come from a title. Instead, you must influence a person and persuade him or her to follow your lead. I clearly failed to influence Alex. The worst part of it was that my two older daughters looked at each other as one of them said, "How stupid were we to stand against the wall when Dad made us do it?" That lesson is also true in life. People will not always follow you because of your title; they will challenge you. And when others observe how you handle those challenges, they will adjust their behavior accordingly. Leadership is influence, nothing more, nothing less.

PEOPLE ARE ALWAYS WATCHING YOU, AND YOU ARE INADVERTENTLY INFLUENCING OTHERS

During a keynote speech I was delivering, I asked the audience two questions. "How many of you own your own business or work in a business?" Everyone raised their hands. Then I asked, "How many of you are in leadership positions?" About two-thirds of the people in the room raised their hands. Even if we do not realize it, each of us is in a position of leadership because someone is always watching what we say and what we do, and in turn, what they observe will influence their decisions.

Between 1996 and 1998, I was the general manager of a Benckiser subsidiary and living in Prague, one of the most enchanting cities in Europe. It was one of the most enjoyable assignments I'd ever had. There, I was able to find the right balance between work and family. We were members of a great church with a vibrant youth group. Kathy and I organized a bunch of activities for the kids, especially for our oldest daughter Jennifer's youth group. One day the kids went off on a capture the flag adventure in a nearby park, but their ammunition was ketchup and mustard. When they emerged from the woods laughing, they were covered in so much junk that we had to hose them off before they could get in the car.

Around 2006, as Facebook was gaining global momentum, I received a friend invitation from a young woman. The message asked, "Are you the Tom Kereszti who lived in Prague?" Well, if you search Facebook, you will find only a handful of people named Kereszti; it was obviously me she was looking for.

I politely answered yes, but I added, "I do apologize, but I do not remember who you are. How can I help you?"

In disbelief, I read her answer: "I just wanted to thank you for changing my life." After I shared this story with Kathy, she said that she remembered the young woman as a member of Jennifer's youth group.

See, people are always watching you, and they will make decisions following your example, based on your actions. Unknowingly, my collective set of actions and statements influenced this woman as a young person to make some major decisions that ultimately changed her life. I do not know if it was the way I interacted with my daughters, my wife, the youth group kids, or other parents, but the bottom line is that she was watching me, and as a result of my influence, she accepted Jesus as her Savior. Lead yourself wisely, because each day your spouse, your kids, your colleagues, your customers, your business partners, and your friends observe what you say and what you do, and although you may not realize it, you're influencing them.

WORTHY CAUSES WILL HELP
YOU INFLUENCE OTHERS

Do you remember where you were on September 11, 2001? I am sure we all do. It was a day that changed our lives forever. I was on my fifth expatriate assignment, and we were living just outside London in Old Windsor at the Manor Farm. Funny, the day we met the real estate agent who was going to show us the house, he got stuck in traffic, so we had to wait forty minutes for him to show up. The house is part of the Crown Estate and has a beautiful view of Windsor Castle. When we were there, it was nothing but fresh air and luscious greens for miles, and so quiet that you could hear the birds and horses nearby.

The day we were moving in, the house all of a sudden began to shake, the windows rattling. Alarmed, Kathy and I looked at each other as if to say, *What the heck is going on?* We went outside and saw a Concord overhead, climbing into the sky, and we learned quickly that our house was directly in the flight path and just ten minutes from Heathrow Airport.

Now if you know anything about the expatriate community, you know that they tend to be very close with everyone knowing each other's business. Most expatriates have families, so the community revolves around the international schools. The nuclei of the community are the spouses, a wonderful group of individuals who hold down the fort while the executives are working 24/7 in one way or another. Kathy used to call her group the corporate widows' club.

On 9/11, I was in Amsterdam in a conference room when word reached us about the World Trade Center. Kathy finally had tracked me down; she was devastated by the news. We'd both grown up in New York City and still knew many people there, including a number of firemen. It was impossible to reach anyone in New York City that day, but we knew our immediate families were okay. I tried to take the first flight back to England, but with all the madness I could not get back until the afternoon of September 12. When I finally got home, I found Kathy glued to the TV, watching Sky News. As she was watching, they showed a picture of Heathrow Airport, and in the background you could see thousands of stranded travelers. A British Airways representative who was being interviewed said, "All flights are suspended. Unfortunately, as it's an act of war, the airlines are not responsible for any travelers."

When a crisis happens, sometimes unexpected new leaders emerge and stand out. During a crisis, the first thought of any leader should be, *How can I help people?* In the midst of bad events, leaders emerge and find good things to do. Now Kathy's gift has always been her giving nature; she is a person who loves to help. And sure enough, she had this overwhelming desire to somehow help the people stranded at Heathrow Airport. Without a plan, she got in her car and drove out to Heathrow to see how she could make a difference. She picked terminal 4, which at the time was the international terminal, and just started asking stranded travelers how she could help them. Two recurring themes emerged from this. First, all hotels were sold out, and people were left to sleep on the airport floors without showers. Second, some people were at the end of their vacation, very low on funds, and did not have the means to buy a meal. If you have ever been to Heathrow Airport, you know the exorbitant prices for everything.

Suddenly the light went on in Kathy's head. Most of the expatriates we knew had sizable houses with spare bedrooms, full refrigerators, and warm showers. She fired up the school phone tree and started what eventually became a viral campaign to see who would host the stranded American travelers until flights were resumed. Within a few hours, the school bus made it to terminal 4, and Kathy loaded it up with stranded travelers. The bus then drove back to the school parking lot, and the host families picked everyone up and took them home. By the next day, as word spread, the momentum grew. We had three American schools in the region. My girls attended TASIS, the American International School in England, which is where the initiative started. There was also the American School in London and ACS in Cobham.

Kathy's circle of influence was expanding with three schools stepping up, which meant a lot more volunteers, more host families, and more school buses. In the end we were able to house hundreds of stranded Americans. I think it was the second day or so, but British Airways got wind of our efforts and tracked Kathy down at the airport. They gave her a badge and said, "Whatever you need form British Airways, just let us know." In the midst of the 9/11 crisis, they had provided a civilian a temporary badge giving her access to Heathrow Airport. Now that is influence. But if you think about it, you'll conclude that it made a lot of sense. If you were British Airways with thousands of frustrated people yelling at you every minute, wouldn't you be accommodating to the folks who had just shown up like knights in shining armor to ease your headache and take away your problems?

And Kathy's influence kept building. I think it was about the third day, when flights resumed, that Kathy's phone rang. It was Virgin Atlantic on the other end. We do not recall ever asking Virgin for help, yet here they were informing Kathy that they had a 747 with open seats leaving for New York City in four hours. All we had to do was get the people to Heathrow in time.

Some wonderful stories evolved over these few days, like when Kathy had just met a woman who was frantic with two young boys. It turned out she was just returning from Russia, where she had adopted twin boys. With the language barrier, she was not able to speak with them to explain the situation, and the boys were very upset. Kathy quickly dialed her Russian friend Vicky and put her on the cell phone. Vicky was able to talk with the boys in Russian, which caused everyone to calm down.

Our Good Samaritan story made the news. An elderly British woman Olive called Kathy, also wanting to help, and ended up hosting two young American girls. When flights resumed, the two girls extended their stay to share afternoon tea with Olive a few more days. Great, lifelong relationships were built.

See, leadership is influence, and everyone has the opportunity to influence others when rallied for a worthy cause. Kathy didn't have a title or the corner office, she did not have a huge budget, and she didn't have political connections. She just had a heart to help, and she stepped out of her comfort zone to lead a worthy cause. People will buy into you and rally behind worthy causes. Helping others in need is something we all love to do.

IF YOU ARE HUMBLE AND GENUINE, YOU WILL INFLUENCE OTHERS

Dr. Frank Morelli was one of my mentors and my boss at Colgate-Palmolive. He taught me that just because you're high up in the food chain doesn't mean you can't be a genuine person, treat others with respect, or make fun of yourself. Frank hired me as a manager on his team. It was my first job at corporate headquarters. I had an office in New York City overlooking Park Avenue and the Waldorf Astoria. I learned a lot from Frank over the next few years, most importantly that it was not about me and the Park Avenue view. Frank was a great business mind and a servant leader.

I recall the first time I was invited to Frank's house for dinner. We started with a quick tour of his house. Now I had just purchased my first two-bedroom condo, so Frank's house impressed me with its sheer size, not to mention the cathedral hallway, the formal dining room, and of course his home office with a massive desk and wall unit. I said to myself, *It's good to be a VP. Someday it will happen for me.*

After I'd had several drinks, Mother Nature called, and Frank directed me to the downstairs hallway bathroom. To my astonishment, hanging above the toilet was his PhD diploma. When

I sat back down at the dinner table, I could not help myself from asking Frank, "Why in God's name would you hang your diploma over the toilet instead of in your beautiful office?" Frank simply replied, "If I hang it in my office, no one will see it, but because it's over the toilet, just about everyone who comes to my house will see it." That is the kind of man Frank was, down to earth, real, and humble, a person who could come up with creative solutions and who was a brilliant executive. He was a servant leader before that became a buzz phrase. I wish that everyone could have a Frank in their lives or that they become a Frank in someone else's life.

INFLUENCE THROUGH FAITH

Only a few people are outspoken about their faith, but many are inspired and influenced by divine causes. I have found that most business leaders, regardless of their status, industry, or location, are open to biblical ideas and discussion. Never has anyone refused to accept when I offered to lead in a prayer for them, their family, or their business.

CEO roundtables and masterminds are well-known. As I contemplated the next phase of my life and my career, I explored Christian-based opportunities like C12 and Convene, finally choosing to join the John Maxwell's team of independent coaches. I found it a unique opportunity to help businesses with their challenges and at the same time model biblical business principles. But more on this topic in chapter 7.

As I grew and matured as a servant leader, I found joy in giving back and helping businesses make a difference to their customers, employees, partners and stakeholders. Today I have the honor of serving the Rock Church in San Diego, leading their roundtable business ministry, equipping many business leaders to integrate their faith with their business practices. It is giving back and making a difference with a lifetime of experience and by divine appointment.

TO INFLUENCE OTHERS, YOU MUST TAKE THE LEAD

I had leadership qualities even at young age growing up in Budapest, Hungary. I could talk to anybody about anything, and I regularly gave my grandmother fits because I would arrive two hours late from school. Back in those days, growing up in Hungary was safe. My elementary school was about a thirty-minute trolley ride away. As early as the fourth grade I was making the commute on my own. I would walk down the hill from my apartment in the hills of Buda, take the trolley four stops, then walk up the hill to my elementary school.

I was always disciplined in the morning about getting to school on time, but on the way home I always got distracted, talking to people or getting into a pickup game of soccer. I was born in 1956. In the early 1960s, soccer was still vibrant in Hungary. The influence of the legendary Puskás era, the 1954 World Cup, and the 1964 Olympic gold medal still had the country gaga over soccer. I was probably in sixth grade, when on the way home from school I stopped off at the local park for a game of soccer.

It was a magical sunny day. I got into the game as a substitute and made the most of it. I was too short to be a forward, so I played midfield, feeding the ball and even scoring a few times. I found myself as a ten-year-old playing with guys sixteen years of age and older who were much bigger than I. Yet as the game progressed, I found that they were putting more and more confidence in me as I set up plays, feeding them the ball and leading them into battle. Looking back, it was one of my first leadership experiences. In a very short period of time, initially not knowing many of the kids, all of a sudden I was leading them.

Leadership lesson #1 is that if you want to influence others, don't be afraid to step up. When there is a lack of leadership, many people are afraid to step up. See, when opportunity presents itself, you need to rise to the occasion. I had the opportunity; I took the lead, and all the other kids followed. Whenever there is a leadership vacuum, someone has to fill it, so why not you? If you want to influence others, the first thing you must do is step out of your comfort zone and take the lead. If you sit on the sidelines, a leadership opportunity will never come to you.

COMMON SENSE MAKES IT EASIER
TO INFLUENCE OTHERS

Bart Becht was the CEO at Benckiser when I first joined the company. After a few months, my boss left the company, and I reported directly to Bart for almost a year before a new VP was named. This time gave us the opportunity to get to know each other. What I found made Bart unique was his common sense. Benckiser was known at the time as one of the premier consumer goods marketing companies, and there was an abundance of accomplished marketers who knew more than Bart. But Bart would always outsmart them with a combination of marketing know-how and common sense.

One time he and the rest of our team were analyzing the results of a product launch—a spot cleaner—and trying to determine why the product was not selling as expected. Bart got up in front of the room, drew a dot on the board designating a stain on an article of clothing, and said, "Look, it's pretty simple." He took the bottle of spot cleaner, aimed the nozzle at the dot, and pulled the trigger. Well, the cleaner sprayed out, making a big circle around the dot, but nothing hit the bull's-eye, which was the placeholder for the stain. Bart said, "That is why we're not selling this product. Customers are not stupid." While everyone else at the company was busy analyzing our media results and other market indicators, Bart simply pointed out that the trigger was misaligned and therefore missed shooting the stain, which is the first thing our customers would notice. Our consumers may have been willing to try the spot cleaner once, but they wouldn't make a second purchase. I learned from Bart that marketing products is not rocket science. It starts with simple common sense and a knowledge of human behavior.

YOU MUST BE INTENTIONAL IF YOU ARE TO INFLUENCE OTHERS

In 1991, I was working for Colgate-Palmolive in a midlevel management position. I reported to Dr. Frank Morelli, who to this day remains one of three bosses I deeply respect. Frank practiced servant leadership, and he always viewed people as customers or team members. I can recall no time that he spoke adversely of anyone or any situation. For some reason Frank recognized my potential and, over a three-year period, invested in my development, always encouraging me, always putting me into situations where I had a good chance to succeed.

Colgate hired C. K. Prahalad from the University of Michigan as a consultant to work with a group of executives to help with our long-term strategic plan. Frank put me on the team, and I took every opportunity to learn and to help others. The experience also allowed me to interact with many senior leaders in the company. CK helped us take inventory of our brand equity, and we came up with different categories of strategies to leverage our strengths and help identify investment priorities. As a result of this long-term strategy, the oral care category with the flagship Colgate brand became our number one priority. In less than ten years after that strategy meeting, Colgate-Palmolive overtook Procter & Gamble as the #1 global oral care company.

Frank continued to invest in me. One of the keys to leadership is intentionality. You must be intentional in your plans if you are to succeed. A little luck always helps, but no one gets ahead by accident. I recall after a meeting with some C-level executives, Frank and I created a plan that I would present to four of the senior executive vice presidents of the company. But as a first step, Frank said, "We are sending you to speech classes." At the time I spoke with a heavy New York accent and at lightning speed, so it was very difficult for other people to understand me. I recall being in a meeting with Bill Cooling, a senior executive vice president, and although I thought my questions made a lot of sense, Bill had to repeat what I'd said to make sure he understood just what the heck I was asking. I worked with Eileen, who is a very skilled public speaking coach, for almost a year. I am forever thankful for her patience.

It took me many more years to become a confident and polished speaker. Frank put me on several high-profile projects, and we did complete our plan, which I did present to several executive vice presidents, including Ed Field, who was in charge of international business development. See, Frank "loaned me" his influence, and in turn this allowed me to begin to influence others.

In 1991, as the Iron Curtain was unraveling, most every multinational company was quickly entering Eastern Europe, and naturally they were all looking at their employee base for native speakers of the languages in the Eastern Bloc. Thank God I was born in Hungary and not in Poland, or else you probably would not be reading *C Suite and Beyond* now. As luck would have it, out of twenty thousand employees worldwide, only four spoke

Hungarian. Now I had just completed presenting to several senior executive vice presidents, and I was still fresh in their minds.

With Frank's help, we set up a meeting with Ed Field, and shortly after that, I had my first expatriate assignment. I moved to Budapest to help start up Colgate-Palmolive Hungary. See, if I had not taken advantage of the opportunity that Frank had given me and been noticed by the executive VPs, then I never would have been considered for that expatriate assignment. But I had taken advantage, had stepped up, and was ready when the opportunity came. If you start preparing when the opportunity arises, it is too late, and the opportunity will pass you by. So exert your influence every chance you have; step up and rise to the occasion. See, in order to influence others, it takes some time. It was almost a two-year process for me. But when opportunity knocks, you'd better be ready.

TO INFLUENCE OTHERS, YOU MUST LEAD BY EXAMPLE

It was an ordinary day in 1968 when my mom came home and simply said, "I got married, and we are moving to New York." Like any child at age twelve would be, I was both excited and scared. We arrived at JFK airport with a couple of suitcases that contained everything we owned. Without being able to speak a word of English, we moved into a new neighborhood. Being an outgoing kid, when I saw a bunch of guys playing outside, I went out to join them. The language barrier was something to overcome, but they were bent on teaching me some English. I was very excited when I came home and shared the first English word I had learned: *shit.* My mom quickly came to understand that she had better get me an English tutor if this was going to work.

After a month of English lessons, I headed off to my first day of school at a local Catholic elementary school, Queen of Martyrs. Now in those days the school uniform was blue slacks, white shirt, and a blue and green checkered tie. My grandfather spent days teaching me how to make a proper tie knot, so I wasn't going to wear a clip-on tie. In my first two weeks of school I quickly realized why clip-on ties were more popular—because they are practical.

This was in 1968, before we had the term *bullying.* In those days many people still subscribed to the survival of the fittest mentality. One day about two weeks into school, some of the other kids figured out I was easy prey because I did not speak English well. Each day we would have recess in the schoolyard, and one day this group of kids came up to me, grabbed me, and put about six tight knots into my necktie through the fence. I was helpless because I could not get those knots out, and suddenly I realized why clip-on ties were a genius idea. Once recess was over, I remained stuck for about five minutes, when a nun finally rescued me and cut me loose from the fence. Needless to say, this was a low moment in my life, very embarrassing—and just a few months after arriving in New York.

The following week at recess, I saw the same group of guys walking toward me. I knew this was not going to end well, so it was time for me to do a gut check. Did I want to be embarrassed again, or would

I prefer to stick up for myself? When the guys got close enough, I bull-rushed the biggest one, throwing him to the ground. Frankly I do not remember who won the fight. It did not matter, though; I had stood up for myself, and they knew that if they were going to pick on me again, it would cost them.

The biggest guy was named Louis Manthis. By the end of seventh grade he had become my wingman and I had become the leader of the pack. I made sure that as a group, we would never bully others. Sure, we had fun as all young boys do, and we got into plenty of trouble, especially with the nuns, who regularly disciplined kids by giving them a good beating—and we got more than our fair share of those—but because I was now the leader, I could choose the direction.

In eighth grade our music teacher asked for volunteers for the Christmas midnight mass choir. I always loved singing, so I raised my hand, and quickly Louis, Robert, and the rest of our gang put their hands up as well. Sister Gloria just about fell over, thinking it was a miracle that the mischief-making troublemakers (not exactly the Vienna choirboys) had volunteered to join her. When Louis, Robert, and I walked down from the balcony at midnight mass to the font of the church to taking Communion, it was priceless to see the nuns' faces, a picture of utter amazement. Yes, miracle do happen. See, to influence others, you must stand up for yourself and for what is right. In order to change others and get them to follow you, you have to lead by example.

IT'S EASIER TO INFLUENCE OTHE...
YOU ADOPT THEIR PERSPECTIVE

Erez Vigodman was CEO of the Strauss Group when he hired n...
to lead Strauss's international coffee division. I spent a lot of time
with Erez and found him to be not only a brilliant strategist but also
a person who understood people. That was his biggest gift; he was
a person whisperer. Strauss Group had a consolidation strategy to
acquire emerging market coffee roasters, and as a result we spent
a lot of time in smoke-filled conference rooms, eating rich foods
and sharing drinks with representatives of the companies we were
trying to acquire in Eastern Europe and Latin America.

One of our acquisitions was located in Serbia, and everyone on
our team was concerned with getting at least a 51 percent majority
share of the company. Erez, showing his ability to adopt the
seller's perspective, said something simple. Darko, who owned the
company at the time, was in his late thirties. He loved fancy cars,
beautiful women, and his freedom. He was king of his small hill,
proud of his accomplishment, and did not want to lose control. Erez
knew that in the end Darko would sell because Darko would never
want to be part of a large, structured organization.

We finalized the deal as an equal fifty-fifty partnership. It was going
to be only a matter of time before Strauss gained the majority. Erez
was correct in his assessment, and his agreeing to enter into the
acquisition without having the majority share was a risk that paid off.
Darko cashed out in about five years and sold Strauss the remainder,
so now Strauss had a controlling interest in the company.

u want to positively influence others? I would encourage you to ask yourself a few questions:

- *What are the three most important things you want to achieve through your influence?*

- *Do you have a list of people you want to influence?*

- *How can you help those people you want to influence?*

- *What is your plan of influence, and how can you help assert your influence?*

- *Do you have a noble or divine cause people can get excited about?*

- *Do you ask questions and listen for understanding to gain the other persons perspective?*

2

THE FOUR KEYS TO LEADERSHIP SUCCESS

It was July 1996, and we had reservations for ten people at Kampa Park, my favorite restaurant in Prague, which offers a beautiful setting along the Vltava riverbank beneath the shadow of the historic Charles Bridge. Kathy and I arrived a few minutes early to make sure we had time to review the seating arrangement one last time and to place a small gift for each of the spouses and colleagues on the table. Even though Kathy and I were the newcomers, we wanted to make each person feel welcome and thank them in advance for their efforts in light of the big challenges ahead. Breaking bread together, sharing food and wine (or in the case of Prague, great beer), is a tradition as old as humanity. This occasion would give us an opportunity to take a breather from the stress of the business, get to know each other, and enjoy our spouses in an informal setting. I wanted to send two messages: first, I wanted to let my colleagues know that they and their spouses were appreciated, and second,

I wanted to communicate the fact that before we could lavishly celebrate, we first had to fix a struggling business.

The good Lord truly blessed me with my third expatriate assignment. Prague is one of the most beautiful cities in the world, and Reckitt Benckiser is a great company. At that time, the company was still Benckiser, and they had recruited me to turn around their CSR (Czech and Slovak Republic) subsidiary. By then I had established myself as a turnaround specialist in the Eastern European consumer goods industry. At the time, the local subsidiary had stopped growing and was bleeding profusely at the bottom line. The company sales were about $42 million with operating losses of about $1.6 million. By 1999, when I was asked to lead Benckiser's Mexican subsidiary, company sales soared to $64 million with operating profits in excess of $4 million. So what led to this turnaround?

Benckiser's offices were located in downtown Prague, just a short walk from Old Town on Voršilská Street. Prague is like a fairy tale city in a book you read as a small child with princes and princesses in palaces and castles. Everything in Prague was enchanting, including our offices, which were in the residence of a former prince. The only thing that was not enchanting were the business results.

When I took over the business, everyone was in panic mode. Already in July, they had realized the annual sales and profit plan were both unattainable. The former general manager, who had come from sales, spent 90 percent of his time running around the country selling volume at huge discounts. He may have been a good salesperson, but he didn't have a clue how to lead a company. Simply put, the people were without direction and were selling the wrong products, offering excessive discounts, working on the wrong priorities, spending money on the wrong activities, and doing business in a panic. How does a company fall into such a downward spiral? Over the years I have always been able to break performance down into four keys that lead to a company's either thriving or struggling. Let's use this turnaround example as a case study of the four keys to leadership success.

The first key is company culture. Every thriving company I've ever worked for had a unique culture. For every company I have turned around, its culture was the first thing I looked at. This company did indeed have a culture, but unfortunately it was not a unique culture, and it was full of panic and "I don't know what to do." So how does one turn this into a winning approach?

I started by defining values that everyone in the company could embrace. There is no right or wrong culture, just the presence or absence of a culture. Apple's culture is very different from Microsoft's. Both are great companies, but they each have a different personality.

Our company culture was based on entrepreneurship along with financial responsibility. I wanted my team to embrace an ownership mindset focused on achievement and mutual respect. I, as a leader, had to make sure to create an environment that supported these values. For example, if I wanted a culture of entrepreneurial achievement, I had to make sure we created a fail-safe environment where effort was prioritized much more highly than someone's getting it wrong; those who excelled on their own initiative had to be rewarded. If I wanted an ownership mindset with financial responsibility, we needed a compensation structure to reward behavior in line with that mindset. Benckiser had a great bonus compensation structure by having local teams focus on three key performance indicators: sales, profits, and net working capital. If the team exceeded expectations on all three indicators, they could earn bonus of up to 120 percent of their base salary. Now that is putting your money where your mouth is.

Finally, respect was a value everyone had to exhibit. We had to walk the talk in respecting each other, our customers, and our suppliers. We had to respect people's time, along with everyone's opinion and input, and we had to value each other. Diverse ideas were encouraged, which led to plenty of debates, but any debate had to be done respectfully, and I always had the final vote. Once we decided on something, everyone had to support it; there was no room for dissension.

My first priority was to create confidence and build relationships.

When I was a junior manager working at Colgate-Palmolive, the company had just hired Larry Wagner as senior vice president. During his first three days, Larry very informally invited us to gather around his office, where he simply introduced himself. He shared with us his values, told us a little about what made him tick and what he hoped to do, and asked us for our help in advance. He acknowledged up front that he did not have all the answers and that he was looking to us to help make things happen. I thought to myself, *What a breath of fresh air. In my six-year tenure at Colgate, I have never seen this. Here is a senior executive, informal, down to earth, rolling up his sleeves and reaching out to everyone.* It is a formula I have been following since.

So naturally when I first arrived in Prague, I called everyone around the office in the front foyer. and simply introduced myself and my values, said a little about my family and my achievements, and asked everyone to help make our journey a success. A few weeks later I did the same at our sales meeting with the sales team.

Now if I were to ask people to help me, I also had to let them know how they could help. To my surprise, a company-wide communication system was nonexistent, and we did not even have something as simple as a daily sales report. So that is the first thing we implemented, a daily sales report, where everyone in the company received an update each day showing our sales goal for the month, where we were each day, and how much we had yet to go. Over the next few months, we did have employee turnover, but in three years, I let only two people go. Everyone else left on their own.

Early on as our culture started taking hold, one of our midlevel managers had just quit, so I conducted an exit interview with him. I asked him why he was leaving, and his answer was that it was no longer fun working here because everyone was focused on making our plan work. See, once you establish the culture and you lead by example, people figure out pretty quick if they do not belong, and if they don't belong, they leave on their own.

By December 1996 we had made some improvements, but the company's operating profits were still disappointing and we were still in the red. Romana, our CFO, approached me because she was thinking about canceling the company Christmas party. I said, "I am not Scrooge. We should celebrate Christmas." But I also wanted to set the right tone, so we had a low-key Christmas party at a nice venue, limiting it to employees only to keep the costs down. It was a nice event. I said a few kind words, thanking everyone, and used one of my favorite Mother Teresa quotes.

Fast-forward one year to December 1997. Our business had gained momentum with double-digit sales growth and positive operating profit. It was time to celebrate. I wanted to send a very different message from the year before. Planet Hollywood had just opened in Prague, and I decided it would be the perfect venue for our Christmas party, inviting employees, spouses, and friends. Boy, were a lot of tourists disappointed when they learned that Planet Hollywood was closed to the public for the evening. I wanted our team to experience that when you win, you can celebrate your success together in grandiose style. What a party, good food, great music, top-shelf liquor, and people dancing late into the night, having a blast.

I asked Romana, my CFO, to purchase three Planet Hollywood leather bomber jackets so we could honor three employees who had made a big difference that year. I was never one to scold people, instead preferring to recognize and reward outstanding achievement. This was the perfect time to single out a few people in front of their peers and award them for going the extra mile. We selected two people from marketing and one from sales. I opened with a thank-you, stating, "What a difference a year makes." First I thanked all our employees for their hard work and recognized our company's achievement. I also thanked the spouses for their support and recognized them because they had contributed to our success. I know how much Kathy had done to support me and our family while I was working long hours and traveling. I wanted everyone in the room to know that our company efforts and our success was meaningless unless we could celebrate our achievements with our loved ones.

I then called up each of the three award recipients individually and highlighted how they embodied our values of entrepreneurship, taking initiative, and getting other people's support, also mentioning the value their individual projects had brought to the company. Then I hugged each person and handed them their gift.

Tomas was one of our star brand managers who had received a jacket. He had a huge smile on his face, and he wore that jacket the rest of the night with no one able to wrest it away from him. See, just a few years prior, people in Eastern Europe were paying $100 or more for a pair of Levi's jeans. The leather bomber jacket—and the recognition—was a symbol of Western success, so it was priceless. In one short year, we were able to create a winning culture of entrepreneurship that our employees fully embraced and celebrated.

The second key is vision. All successful companies have a clear and simple vision that sets the priorities for their decision-making.

Benckiser's corporate vision was clear in its suggesting an entrepreneurial spirit in regard to creating premium specialty cleaning products. Benckiser originated in Germany and historically focused on water-softening products as German water was rich in calcium and other minerals that made it tough to clean with.

When I started asking about our vision at the local level, no one could tell me with certainty what our vision was, and our actions were clearly not aligned with the corporate direction. At least 80 percent of the company's focus was on a high-volume, low-profit laundry detergent category with the only two specialty products making up less than 10 percent of our sales. Lack of vision usually leads to poor decision-making. See, vision is about the long term, not about this year's budget or even a three-year strategic plan. You do not change your vision every five years; your vision will be the same in twenty or thirty years.

The example I like to use is Coca-Cola, whose slogan is an extremely simple and easy to understand statement: "We refresh the world." If you are an employee, customer, or supplier of Coca-Cola, you know it's about refreshing drinks—with global implications. That is easy to understand and rally behind. We at Benckiser needed to do the same. We needed to rally behind a vision that focused on specialty cleaners, thereby creating a niche segment in the laundry and household cleaning industry.

During the first month after I had arrived, we had a pre–budget planning meeting that was spearheaded by Paul and our marketing team. About an hour into the meeting, I had to interrupt and halt the discussion. Before anything else could be discussed, we had to spend some time coming to an agreement about our vision. It would have been senseless to work on any budget or plan without having a clear and simple vision we all agreed to. The meeting was delayed a few extra days, but we finally reached a consensus, at which point we were ready to discuss opportunities, plans, and projects. Please keep in mind that this was a relatively straightforward exercise. As Benckiser already had a real identity and a focused corporate vision, our task was relatively easy. We did not have to create a new vision, which usually take months, not days, for a company. All we had to do was to own that vision and adapt it to the local market. It was equally important with the vision, as with the company culture, not to have dissension.

When I'd first arrived, the company did not have a sales director but, instead, two sales managers. Peter was in charge of the rapidly growing multinational key accounts, although at the time, key account sales represented only about 35 percent of the mix. I eventually promoted Peter to sales director. One main reason was that he had gotten on board early and bought into the culture and vision we all had agreed on. The other gentleman did not, and as a result he never felt comfortable with our plans or with the other team members. His discomfort led to needless debates and disagreements, and by December 1996, he moved on to a new opportunity.

Once you have a clear vision, unfortunately not everyone will buy into it. However, when employees do not sign on to the culture, values, and vision, they will quickly move on to other opportunities. If they do not move on, you have no other choice but to break ties with them, or else it will be like a cancer eating away at your organization. Culture, values, and vision are never negotiable. You can have all the debate you want before you agree on them, but once they are set, you must either be on board or else get off the train.

The third key is a growth strategy aligned with the company vision. Many companies make the mistake of not aligning their growth plan to their vision, and some companies do not even have a clear vision. When I arrived at Benckiser, there was a clear absence of a company vision, so the strategic growth plan was not exactly strategic. Although this example is specific to one company's cleaning products portfolio, the principles work for any industry. With the focus on low-profit detergents, our local subsidiary was wasting scarce financial resources and spending the sizable media budget supporting a promotional-driven detergent category.

At our first budget meeting, we agreed that our vision would focus on creating premium specialty cleaning products. From this point forward, it was pretty much straightforward when determining how and where we would invest our resources. The strategic planning process became much easier as we agreed where the focus must be. We started with a classic Boston matrix approach, prioritizing our brands and products into the four segments.

We had a lot of discussion on one sensitive topic as detergents made up close to 80 percent of our sales. Everyone was hesitant to make significant changes. This is human nature; most people are afraid to buck the status quo even if it is not working. They say the definition of insanity is doing the same things over and over again and expecting different results. But that is the beauty of a clear and simple vision statement. It provides clarity for the purpose decision-making, that is, determining what you should do and what you should not do. For heaven's sake, if everyone is rowing in the wrong direction, please stop the boat; otherwise you will quickly find yourself going over the waterfall. First aim the boat in the right direction, then begin rowing again. Being true to our vision statement, we ultimately agreed that regardless of the brand, detergents were cash cows at best, so some of the products would be divested.

Up to this point, the majority of our advertising budget was being spent on detergents, and after considerable debate, our second major decision was to reallocate the bulk of our media spend to other priorities. We would support detergents primarily out of the promotional budget and establish a trade marketing program focused on multinational key accounts and the co-ops, which were the largest local retail chain. Our detergent advertising investment would focus almost totally on store activities like displays, promotions, endcaps, and flyers with only one short media burst campaign per year. This decision freed up a lot of resources for other products.

We developed a three-year strategic plan that called for the introduction of one new brand each year, and each of these new brands would result in the development of a premium niche category. We allocated resources by committing most of our marketing budget to these new brands. This meant consumer research, developing local advertising copy, and a heavy media spend, which was all expensive stuff. The good news was, we were in Eastern Europe, so relatively speaking, compared to Western Europe or the USA, these projects were still affordable.

There was one more decision we had to make about brands and products that could grow into starts if given the proper nourishment—or otherwise end up in the coffin. Benckiser's flagship product was a water softener additive called Calgon, and its second flagship product was Calgonit, a detergent for an automatic dishwasher. Although the market segments were small in Eastern Europe, we wanted to invest, grow, and capture the lion's share of these markets. Fabric softeners were a more difficult choice as our plans were to eventually turn them into cash generators.

We also developed a similar decision matrix of our customers and how we would invest into different distribution channels. Eastern Europe traditionally did not have large chains outside the cities and relied more heavily on wholesalers supplying small-format stores. However, this landscape was changing quickly with the emergence of multinational chains like Tesco, Ahold, Makro, and Carrefour. This decision also required us to examine our sales team and its structure and how this money was spent. As we classified multinational chains high on our list of investment priorities, we also established a key account and a trade marketing team to support specific customers way of doing business. We considered the largest local co-op chain to be a multinational key account, and we treated them that way. Last, we recognized that independent small retailers supplied by traditional wholesalers would rapidly erode, so we moved them to a spot in the divestment matrix with little support over the three years.

After we had revised the budget presentation and financials several times, we eventually presented what we had to the regional team and then to the senior executive team. Our three-year strategic plan passed with flying colors. Now it was time for execution.

I have always been a hands-on person, and on average I spent one day each week visiting customers. By early 1997 I had made my first round of visits with our customers, and to each I had conveyed a simple message. I thanked them for their past support, I shared with them our company culture and long-term vision, and I promised them many new exciting initiatives for which we would seeking their help. With our strategic plan approved, it was time to revisit our customers and share our plans.

When it comes to implementation, this is where culture, vision, and strategy come together. It is relatively easy to get customer buy-in when they see you walking the talk of your culture and backing up your vision statement with products and support. With a strong media plan, our customers were just as excited as we were and were eager to load up their stores with our products, anticipating consumer purchases where we all would benefit from this common cause.

The fourth key is a well-functioning team. Just after I joined the company, Paul, my marketing director, came into my office to extend an invitation to a meeting prior to the budget meeting. Our planning meetings usually started off in late August. First we would agree on a first draft, then we would go through several local iterations. After that we would have a regional discussion, before presenting the plan to corporate senior leadership for final approval in late October. The plan would then be approved, or else some fine-tuning would be requested, by early November, which would give the local teams the opportunity to come out with guns blazing in early January.

I thanked Paul and commended him on his initiative to get a jump start on the budget process. Later that afternoon, I stopped in our CFO Romana's office to ask how she was preparing for the meeting. To my surprise, she asked, "What meeting?"

I replied, "Paul is kicking off the budget process with a marketing meeting next week." Romana still had a blank look on her face as she'd had no clue. I later checked with Peter, our sales director, and Peter, our operations manager, and sure enough neither of them had received an invitation either. I already knew the shortfall stemming from a lack of company culture and lack of vision, but I had just learned there was no concept of teamwork.

I went back to Paul the next day and asked, "Don't you think we should invite Romana and the two Peters to your meeting? They would probably give some great input from finance and sales about helping implement your marketing ideas." Paul agreed. Within minutes he had invited both Peters and Romana. What a difference it made to the budgeting process to recognize Paul for his early initiative and also to have the other leaders at the table. Once we kicked off the budget process in late August, we expanded the team and put together a great plan.

As we kicked off the new year, I made it part of my routine to have a meeting with my direct reports every Monday morning for about three hours to discuss what we had learned from the previous week and what challenges or activities we had ahead of us for the coming week. Topics included our sales, our competitors' actions, how our activities were going, and our personnel. It was primarily an opportunity to make sure we were all on the same page and to flag any last-minute issues. It was an idea that came from Rudy Giuliani's book *Leadership*, in which he discusses having done the same with his direct reports while mayor of New York City. If it worked for Rudy, using communication and discipline to run New York City, then I was sure it would benefit our team.

In addition, we also had one planning meeting each month, which we tagged onto the end of our mandatory Monday morning management meetings. We would discuss the next month's activities to make sure we had the right inventory coverage, distribution build with customer support, media plans, etc. It also helped us to reduce our net working capital through better planning.

Last, I also reserved time to meet with each of my direct reports one-on-one, four hours each month. During these one-on-ones, we would review personal or department goals and fine-tune them based on extenuating circumstances. It also gave each person an opportunity to discuss topics of a personal or a business nature.

Each year we also had at least one off-site team building activity for the company, usually centered on our sales meeting. By the end of the second year we had a great team of "mind whisperer" people well-oiled, working together, and supporting each other. All that remained for me as a leader was to equip them, empower them, and get out of their way so they could achieve success. Of course I was always available, and I enabled frequent communications and provided a fail-safe zone where everyone could feel comfortable in case they had to raise issues and speak out.

Well, that is it, the four keys to success. It is where I always look when I am asked to help a company. It is amazing how simplistic all four of these keys seem, yet to get all four right, as simple as they may seem, is a very difficult thing. Many companies overlook one or more of the keys as being unimportant or just do a poor job of leading their organizations each day using these principles.

I promise you that although the case study I have shared with you showcases a consumer goods company in Prague, the same principles hold true globally in any industry. As long as your company is made up of people and sells products to customers, these principles will work.

To help identify your four keys, I would encourage you to ask yourself a few questions:

- *Do I have clearly defined values that guide my life?*

- *Is my vision long term, helping me to make major decisions?*

- *Am I growing in the right areas?*

- *Who are the people surrounding me? Are they supporting me?*

3

KEY #1—WHO ARE YOU?

A PERSON IS DEFINED BY HIS OR HER CHARACTER

> Our ability to handle life's challenges is a measure of our strength of character.
> —*Les Brown*

Someone once wisely said that the only thing that is not buried with a person is their character. A person's character is what defines them. It is how people remember them, almost their legacy. I contend that a person's character is the same as a brand. Brands like Coca-Cola, Nike, and Amazon have a strong and clear identity that we can trust, and they make products that we feel at ease buying. The same is true for a person's identity as we trust them and buy into them.

I remember reading about a Google senior executive, Forrest Hayes, who died of a heroin overdose while with a prostitute, Alix

Tichelman. Here was a man with a beautiful wife, three sons, and two daughters, and that's how his life ended. How does one get to that point? I am not a psychiatrist, but I would think that to get to that point, you must have a major identity crisis. I think if someone had a strong foundation of values, it would prevent them from living such a double life. But that is an extreme example. There are millions of people who are unsure of who they are, what makes them tick, and why they are in a certain relationship or working a particular job. I know several people who lack a strong identity and behave very different depending on the circumstances, such as at being work or being with family or friends.

I must confess, as much as I loved my first expatriate assignment, I underwent an identity crisis when moving back to Hungary for the first time. I was only twelve years old when I emigrated from Hungary to the USA, and returning as an adult, a thirty-year-old executive, was awkward. Every bone in me felt American. My grandmother spoke only Hungarian, and my mom always made it a point to speak to me in Hungarian to preserve the native language. As a side note, my grandmother was also the best cook when it came to the flavors of Hungary; she taught me how to prepare some delicious Hungarian meals. As you can imagine, the topics of conversation with my grandmother when I was young did not lead me to develop the most sophisticated Hungarian vocabulary. I was not prepared for business dialogue or negotiations. It was misleading in that my pronunciation of the Hungarian language did not hint to any shortcomings; it was simply my lack of vocabulary.

At first, I did try to conduct business discussions in Hungarian, but I felt at a major disadvantage and even sounded stupid many times. So I did two things. First, I hired a language tutor to help me build up my vocabulary, so I could hold my own in a business setting. Second, for about a year I conducted all negotiations in English with the help of a translator. That was where the false identity started kicking in. People looked at me as if asking, *Who is this person? Why does he have to speak English when we know he can speak Hungarian? Who does he think he is?*

To complicate my feelings, Jennifer, our oldest daughter, attended the American International School, but when it came time for our middle daughter, Nicole, to start first grade, Kathy, to my surprise, insisted Nicole attend a Hungarian elementary school. Our youngest daughter, Alex, was born in Budapest, in the same hospital I was born in. Kathy sometimes joked that Alex was born not only in the same hospital but also maybe even in the same bed considering her age and the conditions. My relatives and old friends in Hungary had reconnected with me, so my circle of friends included both international and Hungarian families.

A battle was starting to take place inside me, not just about the language but also about who I was. Was I Hungarian, or was I American? Not having a clear identity was an obstacle to our growth, and as a family we had to make a decision. It took some time to sort things out, but ultimately we choose to remain true to our New York roots. We had a fabulous run of fifteen years, living in five different countries as an American expatriate family. We made some wonderful friends in each country, many of whom we remain close to even though we live in different parts of the world.

> The two most important days in your life are the day you are born and the day you find out why.
>
> —*Mark Twain*

As a leader of a team, you must first start by knowing who you are. Like a house that must be built on a strong foundation, a clear identity—who you are and why you get up each morning—is essential. Before you can lead others, first you must learn how to lead yourself. I suggest that in order to effectively lead yourself, you need to honestly answer three questions.

Imagine the three intersecting circles of a Venn diagram. The first circle is knowing who you are, the second is knowing what you are good at, and the third is knowing what you're passionate about. Where these three circles intersect is where you should be living your life. Life's bonus is when you find a market interested in buying the result of you, your passion, and your expertise. Not only will you lead a successful life but a wealthy abundant one. Unfortunately, many people do not have a clear answer, and because of life's pressures, they compromise one or more of the circles, leading to their unhappiness as a result of not living up to their full potential.

It took me many years to find my answer, but now those answers define me. Who am I? I am a servant leader. What am I passionate about? I love making people's lives better. I love adding value to their lives. What am I good at? I am good at leading and mentoring people. The beauty of this formula is that I can use it regardless of the circumstance or situation. The formula works if I am at work, at home with my family, at church, with friends, or on a sports team. I can be a servant leader at work or at home. I can add value to my customers, my spouse, or my friends. I can mentor my employees or my children.

Nick Vujicic is one of the most inspirational speakers I have ever heard. He is a man of faith who was born without arms or legs. Today he is married with three kids, and he has turned away some twenty thousand requests to speak at events. As he tells his story, early on, when he was a young boy, he tried to commit suicide because of his physical limitation and all the bullying he had been subjected to. As he matured, and through his faith, he eventually came to recognize who he was, what he was good at, and what his passion was. Through his calling, he became a global leader speaking out against bullying.

Nick is a master communicator. It is a very valuable experience to watch him onstage with no arms and legs, using the rest of his body to portray his story and to move the audience with laughter and other emotions. Can you picture Nick telling the story of when he first wanted to share his message with schoolkids in Australia, having to dial (on a rotary phone) more than fifty times before one school agreed to have him come speak in front of the students? Or when he was skydiving and was so scared that his knees were shaking?

Nick shares how daunting and challenging it was as he first set out to fulfill his calling. But he knew who he was and what he was passionate about, and over the years he mastered his art as a public speaker. Now he is living his dream. He jokes about how he prays each day for a miracle, that God will give him arms and legs, even keeping a pair of shoes in his closet in case his prayer is answered. Having realized that his physical limitations are part of who he is, Nick leveraged those limitations to give himself a unique identity, become the person he is today, and accomplish his mission.

A person's character is built on his or her values. I believe a person's character evolves over time, but it starts off at a young age where the individual adopts a set of values. It is a lot more difficult to develop new values once you're an adult. My values consist of integrity, honesty, love, respect, faith, humbleness, and hard work. I developed one of my values, honesty, when I was about seven years old. I do not recall all the details, but it began with a confrontation between me and my grandmother. I had said something that was a blatant lie, and my grandfather smacked me so hard that my head bounced off the wall. My grandfather never had smacked me before or after that incident, so what I'd said must have really upset him. This is not to say the smack did not hurt—my grandfather was a strong man, so the smack did hurt—but what hurt more was the realization that what I had said could get someone so upset that he would smack me because of it. So honesty has been one of my values from early on.

See, when you are an adult and when lying becomes one of your daily habits, then dishonesty is a value you come to embrace. I do not want to play party politics, so pick any politician. Whomever you choose, there is a good chance that lying is one of his or her daily habits. When a person is on national TV and says "I do not recall ever lying" or "I did not intend to lie," just what does that mean? The person is just manipulating words to hide the truth.

See, truth is absolute, not relative. But if you think it is relative, then lying is part of your value set. Now I am not here to declare which values are good and which are not. All I'm saying is that each person should have a set of values. If you do not have a set of values, you will be lost in life and will find it difficult to define who you are and what you stand for.

> Humility is to make a right estimate of oneself.
> —*Charles H. Spurgeon*

Being humble is one of my values, and humility is also a quality I value highly in others. Having always sought the guidance of experts, I learned early on in business to establish a circle of advisers. I have always included a trusted attorney as one of the key advisers in my circle. While living in Hungary, I met Kornelia, who is a brilliant attorney. I cherish her friendship to this day. Kornelia has that rare combination of a great legal mind and common sense. Not only can she explain the intent of the law, but also she can offer practical advice on how to solve business problems. She is an advocate and also a humble person who has helped me in many ways, not just as an attorney.

In each country I and my family lived in, we made it a tradition to celebrate Thanksgiving with a diverse group consisting of Americans living abroad and people of other nationalities who had never experienced the holiday. We were preparing to host our Thanksgiving dinner while living in Budapest and were delighted that Kornelia and her Hungarian friend György were going to join us. We had a great evening of feasting, laughing, and drinking till late. Kornelia called me the next day to thank me for a great time and also to thank me for not talking politics and being critical of the current administration. I was taken aback by her comment as I'd had no reason to talk Hungarian politics on Thanksgiving. I asked her why she had mentioned the topic. She confessed that her Thanksgiving guest was the son of the prime minister at the time, József Antall. Most people would have advertised being in the prime minister's inner circle, but Kornelia and György, both humble individuals, had focused on our friendship and enjoying our company instead of on name-dropping. Hungarian culture puts an emphasis on the importance of titles and people's rank in society, so not mentioning their association with the prime minister at a dinner celebration spoke volumes about their humbleness. Being humble does not mean being weak and a pushover, though, as Kornelia was a fierce competitor in the boardroom as well as an accomplished lawyer. A humble individual realizes it is always about something much bigger than just himself or herself.

I am a big New York Giants fan and was fortunate to see Eli Manning lead our team to two Super Bowl victories. Eli is a great example of how to remain humble among the New York fanfare. Allison Stangeby, vice president of community and corporate relations for the Giants, shared a story about Eli: "We go to the hospital, and he doesn't want cameras. He doesn't want anybody there. He just wants to walk around and see the kids and their parents. That's it. There's no fanfare." Now that is keeping it real, especially in today's world of self-obsessed multimillion-dollar athletes.

> If you don't stick to your values when they are being tested, they are not values, they are your hobbies.
> —*Job Stewart*

You can separate values into two buckets. The first bucket is filled with your internal values, the ones you believe in. These are the values you develop early as a child that are inherent to your character and that stay with you for a lifetime. These values, which may be perceived as positive or negative, are hardwired and work almost like muscle memory.

The second bucket is filled with your external values. These are the values that other people perceive through your actions. When you find yourself in a predicament where you must make a decision based on your values, your external values will be evident in how you act. If your internal values line up with your external values, then people will perceive you as having a strong character. They will say you walk the talk.

A disconnect becomes evident when people adopt values based on something that is popular but that it is not part of their internal value set. They will state ownership of a particular value, but in reality, as situations present themselves to test them, their actions will not align with the particular value. Their external values take over, meaning that their words do not match their actions. If your internal values do not line up with your external values, then people will perceive you as a phony.

Let's use integrity as an example. Integrity is a value that is recognized and accepted across all cultures and industries. It is an internal value. Contrast that with your reputation, which is an external value. Integrity describes who you are, whereas reputation describes who others think you are. You build integrity through being, whereas you build your reputation by doing.

Dr. Frank Morelli, a person I had deep respect for, was my boss at Colgate-Palmolive. When you walked in his office, you immediately noticed a plaque on the wall. It simply stated, "Words are cheap. Performance counts." Integrity is built over time and is associated with a person who consistently does what he or she says. People can count on these individuals because their actions speak louder than their words.

I had the honor of serving in a position of leadership for several different companies in different emerging markets of Eastern Europe, the Middle East, and Latin America. Early on in my career I learned the hard way that it was not about me. I remembered Frank Morelli's servant leadership model. I had seen many international executives behaving in a reckless manner. In each of the countries I worked in with an emerging market, there was an aura around expatriate executives that somehow led local businesses and people to try to influence us in the most unorthodox matter.

Soon after I'd arrived at my new expatriate assignment working for Colgate-Palmolive, I had a meeting with the head of an advertising agency. This was common practice for me; within the first two months of taking on a new assignment, I always met with key customers, key suppliers, and key business partners. This meeting was with a reputable international advertising agency, and our company had a global agreement with them. Soon after the meeting, the person in charge of media buying requested a follow-up lunch with me. I agreed, wanting to learn more about the local media buying practices. About halfway through the lunch, this individual told me that it was a common local practice that with each dollar my company invested in media, my personal bank account would profit by 1 percent.

I was floored to have been presented with an outright bribe. It was a test of how my internal and external values lined up. When values direct decisions, choices become much easier. Integrity and honesty are my core values, so I thanked the man for the information and politely declined. It took me awhile to come to grips with what had just taken place with this local subsidiary of an international advertising agency. I wonder how many others with different values may have taken that offer.

> Being powerful is like being a lady. If you
> have to tell people you are, you aren't.
> —*Margaret Thatcher*

I hear people say "I deserve respect" or "I've earned respect." Other times you hear them say, "I am in charge, and it's my way or the highway." Well, if you have to announce you're in charge, that's the clearest signal that you're not. Respect is like grace: someone must give it to you; you cannot ask for it or demand it. And it will come when you least expect it.

I want to let you in on a small secret. Once you find that perfect combination of knowing who you are, what you are good at, and what you are passionate about, you will begin to operate in your strength zone. Challenges will become a lot easier to tackle, and you will automatically earn people's respect.

When I first moved to Budapest on my first expatriate assignment, my uncles, aunts, and cousins were delighted. I was like the prodigal son returning home. Soon after, my uncle invited us to their farm for an honorary pig slaughter. Although this may seem barbaric to some of my American friends, I assure you that it is a common thing in Central European and Eastern European countries. It was a cold Saturday in February. We had gotten an early start to arrive on the farm by 7:00 a.m. Unbeknownst to me, my uncle was the pig expert in town. By the time we arrived, he had already finished off two pigs.

As a young boy I visited the farm many times with my dad before my uncle's house had running water or toilets. Now I must preface this by saying that as a young boy growing up, I did not have a lot of respect for my uncle. I never understood a word he said. He mumbled a lot, and about every fifth word he used was a curse word.

He smoked a ton of unfiltered cigarettes. As I grew older, he always made me drink a shot of the local homemade "moonshine" called Pálinka. So here I was, a grown man and an executive for a Fortune 500 company, visiting my simple-minded uncle.

My uncle selected a huge pig that weighed in about three hundred kilograms, almost six hundred pounds. I will spare you the gory details; let's just say that the process would never have passed FDA inspection. With a few helpers, my uncle lifted this gigantic animal onto a large butcher block table. With nothing but one very sharp knife, my uncle proceeded to dissect the animal with surgical precision. It took him three hours. When he was finished, you could fit the waste into a small brown paper bag. Everything had been processed, cleaned up, and put away in three hours.

I was amazed by his mastery, but what was even more amazing was his silent leadership. Clearly my cousins had been mentored in this process as they and their spouses had sprung into action, knowing the exact timing and what to do at any given point in time, from grinding the meat, to adding spices, to making the salami or pepperoni, and to curing the ham and hanging everything in the smokehouse. As a Colgate executive, I could only wish we had that type of teamwork in our organization.

My lifelong lack of respect for my uncle significantly changed in just a few hours. For the first time, I got to see my uncle in his strength zone. Yes, he still mumbled and he still cursed, but in his strength zone he was a master at his craft, thereby earning my respect. You can earn instant respect by being recognized in your strength zone.

> Trust has two dimensions: competence and integrity. We will forgive mistakes of competence. Mistakes of integrity are harder to overcome.
>
> —*Simon Sinek*

Trust is a foundational value that all people with a strong character possess.

When I first arrived in Budapest on my first expatriate assignment, one day I had lunch at the American International Club. Sitting at the table, I overheard three expatriate spouses having a contest to see who had the best complaint about this godforsaken country their husbands had forced them to live in. Sure, there were some inconveniences in 1992 compared to the infrastructure everyone was used to in the USA, but Budapest, one of the most beautiful cities in Europe, had much to offer. I could not understand why these women were so upset living in a great city like Budapest. As I later learned, there was a lot more to these stories.

A typical daily occurrence would go something like this: The executive goes to work in the morning, and an attractive twenty-five-year-old female colleague, professionally but somewhat skimpily dressed, and with a big smile, eagerly attends to the executive's business needs and does a good job of getting things done. The executive then arrives home after a long day to learn what a difficult day his spouse has had in this godforsaken country with smelly, uncivilized people and antiquated practices. Of course the spouse is exaggerating, but she is agitated about the new country, the language barrier, and the new surroundings.

Now imagine this scenario being repeated just about every day for months, when all of a sudden the executive comes home and informs his wife that he is leaving her for his twenty-five-year-old assistant as their relationship has developed to the point that she is doing more than just taking care of his business problems. Although this scenario happened too many times, many of the marriages survived, having stood the test through strong character and strong values, especially the value of trust. The marriages lacking in trust didn't survive because they failed the character test. The sad part was that the expatriate community was fairly small, so hardly anything could be kept private.

In one instance, a GE executive was having an affair with his assistant, and they were both acting like two high school kids. It was only a short time before the man's wife learned of the affair, and she took it to the next level, starting an affair with the company driver who was assigned to her. Sadly, they became the joke of the community. Shortly after, the executive was fired from his job and his marriage broke up. Had this couple shared a strong identity, strong character, and strong values, the initial affair wouldn't have occurred. Trust is a cornerstone value.

If you have a strong identity, it's easier to build relationships with others. My expatriate assignment in Mexico required a quick learning curve, and in many ways my Eastern European experience had been a good training ground, teaching me how important it was to build relationships. Benckiser had a small presence in the USA, and this was our first market entry in Mexico. I was honored that I had been chosen for this challenge. Benckiser's plan was to establish a small greenfield team, partnering with a local distributor and a local contract manufacturer. This would establish an initial base, and later we would expand by way of local acquisitions to build critical mass.

Paco Cortina, our local distribution partner, was a real gentleman. He and I built a good relationship in a relatively short period of time. I was very respectful of his achievements, and he recognized my skills and the business potential. Paco was very gracious, making warm introductions to all the large retailers in Mexico. Building relationships takes time. This is even more the case in Mexico.

Companies in the USA are more wired to quarterly results and quick action, but it's a different playing field in Mexico. When you're representing a multinational company, it is a given that your products are good. This is where I noticed a lot of Americans in Mexico making a mistake. They spent a lot of time focusing on products, saying how great their company was, how great their products were, and how much money they would invest in their products, but they ignored the fundamentals of human nature. It is funny how many times a group of executives would exit a business meeting high fiving each other, celebrating how they had "killed it," while their Mexican counterparts would simply smile, acknowledge everything, and say, "Let's talk again in a few weeks." Then nothing ever developed, and the Americans were surprised.

In Mexico I found that the local community first wanted to know who it was they were doing business with. They wanted to learn about the person's character. I called it the Mexican dance. In my experience, the first step was to romance each other—go on a few dates and determine if we wanted to do business with each other. This obviously involved spouses, because what better way to learn something about you than when you are together with your wife? Paco, my friend, was a true partner. He took the initiative to invite me to his house one Saturday. As Paco explained to me, he'd also invited some friends, some colleagues, and some buyers for large retailers to introduce me to the local business community.

Mexico City truly redefines what it means to be fashionably late. Kathy and I arrived about 2:00 p.m., as the invitation indicated, which was obviously way too early. Paco was in the backyard preparing a pan of paella, the pan being about three feet in diameter and one foot deep. His arms were yellow up to his elbows in saffron. As I glanced around the backyard, under three very large tents I saw people setting up some large tables with enough seating for about two hundred people. I thought that I would love to see the venue set up for a quinceañera if this was my welcoming and introduction party.

I will never forget Paco's jolly manner while preparing the paella. He turned to me and asked, "Tom, do you know what it takes to make a great paella?" Not sure, I passed on answering. Paco said, "Simply money." He said that the better the ingredients, the better the dish. Now this was a serious paella with chicken breast, chorizo, lobster, shrimp, chilies, and some other great stuff in massive proportions. I was getting hungry just looking at it.

Fashionably late, the guests started arriving around 4:00 p.m. After some opening words from Paco, welcoming everyone and giving a brief introduction, we sat for dinner around 6:00 p.m. Language was a barrier, so I had asked Paco not to put me in the spotlight, preferring to informally mingle with the other guests. Paco had the dinner set up as a self-serve buffet, and Kathy and I walked up together to load up our plates with modest portions. With my Hungarian heritage I love hot peppers, so I had a generous serving of chilies on my plate. I noticed a number of eyes following us as we sat down. My food was very tasty, so after I'd finished, I went back up for seconds, also helping myself to another portion of chilies.

After we finished our food, I started making the rounds at the different tables. I knew I was on the right track after a number of guests told me they'd never seen a gringo eat so many hot chilies. It was a great opening salvo, and it weakened the barriers to facilitate some fun discussions. As the party started to break up, I looked at my watch and saw it was after midnight. We'd had a great time. I was paid another compliment from several of the guests who were locals. They said that gringos would usually come, say hello, and leave early, so they were thankful that Kathy and I had stayed to get to know everyone. I simply replied, "It was our pleasure. With such a great event, along with great people, great food, and great stories, why would anyone want to leave early?"

After this event, many doors opened to me, and I was off to building a successful business in Mexico.

It is difficult to judge character. In fact, I never judge people, only situations. But I am like my friends in Mexico, who wanted to know who they were doing business with, what my character was made up of, and what my values were. Once they understood who I was, they found it to be a much easier decision to buy in to me, Benckiser, and our products, so they gave us their support. In one short year, one of our specialty cleaners had risen to become number one market share in Mexico. Yes, it took a lot more than just a few plates of hot chilies to get to number one, but forming relationships was a strong start.

> Culture eats vision for lunch.
> —*John Maxwell*

A company is defined by its culture. The corporate equivalent of an individual person's character is the company culture. In 2001 I was recruited by the Strauss Group to lead their international coffee division called Elite International. Our business primarily focused on coffee in emerging markets with an additional small business in the Netherlands and France. You may have a similar reaction as I did when they first called. "Who is the Strauss Group?" I was pleasantly surprised to learn that Strauss, with sales over $1 billion, is the leading food company in Israel, like Kraft in the USA or Unilever in Europe. They have joint ventures with three large multinational companies, Danone, Unilever, and Pepsi, and ventures with many other local companies.

Strauss has a rich history. It is owned by a third-generation family, one of the more influential families in Israel. I was the first non-Israeli appointed to run a division of the company, and I was not even Jewish, so it was a unique opportunity. Erez, my boss, formally announced my appointment during a major Strauss event. As Kathy and I were sitting in the large arena, Erez, up on the podium, spoke in Hebrew. The only thing I understood was my name being called. Later that evening there was a reception at the Strauss residence, where I was introduced to colleagues, business partners, and friends. As I was engaged in conversation, Kathy very excitedly grabbed me and said, "You have to come with me and meet Shimon Peres." Talk about influence.

I had a wonderful three years working with the Strauss family, during which I took the time to discover Israel. I had to be in Tel Aviv one weekend each month for board meetings, which gave me an opportunity to see the historical sites. Strauss had facilities in Tel Aviv, Nazareth, Haifa, Ramat Gan, and Achihud, providing me a sneak peek into history every time I visited any of them. I also took an unforgettable private tour of Jerusalem. Being a Christian, I found that seeing this city was monumentally significant to my life. From the Stations of the Cross, to Jesus's tomb, to the underground remains of David's temple, to the Wailing Wall, it all took my breath away. Our family vacation in Eilat was also spectacular, with gorgeous gulf water surrounded by Jordan, Egypt, and the desert. Taking a break from freezing Europe, we enjoyed the warm sunshine, dolphins, camels, water sports, desert tours, and New Year's Eve 2001.

I had many challenges setting the new direction for Strauss's international division, but Erez also asked for my help establishing the future strategy for the Strauss group. To give you an understanding the evolution of Strauss, from the 1930s through the 1960s, the company flourished because of the organic growth of the dairy business that Richard and Hilda Strauss had founded. Michael Strauss, leading the second generation of the family, brought in the new era of cultivating growth through joint ventures and acquisitions. Over the next twenty years, Strauss became a collection of companies and joint ventures all operating separately and functioning under one management team.

In 1997 the Strauss family took majority control of Elite, a company with its own sizable, separate infrastructure. As the Strauss family embarked on the new millennium, it had a collection of companies, each with its individual legacy and culture, and no unifying identity. If the Strauss family were going to continue their success into the third generation, they had to evolve into one culture and streamline the different companies, bringing them under one roof.

I recall a lively heated discussion in Tel Aviv with many of my fellow senior executives from different business units discussing the right culture for our company. Since the Strauss and Elite business units had the largest number of representatives in the room, it was natural for each group to think their culture was the right one. Not sensing any room for compromise, one executive asked why the company could not have two cultures. I finally chimed in, saying first that I was surprised this discussion was taking place now and not in 1998, right after the merger had taken place. Second, I shared that in my twenty years of experience, I had never seen a successful company without a unique positive culture.

Having two cultures is like having a person with multiple personality disorder, not knowing who they are at any given time. Culture is the DNA that binds a company together, giving it purpose. Without a culture, a company is like a person who has no soul. Establishing a company culture begins with shared values. At Strauss we agreed on five values as the foundation of our culture. They were as follows:

1. *Caring* about our consumers, employees, and partners and the communities we operated in.

2. *Daring* to act bravely, taking risks to advance significant change.

3. Having a *passion* for creating foods to delight and nourish others.

4. Taking *responsibility* to advance our vision, reaching our consumers and society as a whole.

5. Having winning *teams*, where every player was seen as a key player and where team members were treated with trust and mutual respect.

Successful organizations understand they must preserve and nourish their culture, because if they do not, a new dominant culture will rise up and take over the company. As with natural selection, if there is a culture vacuum, something will fill it, so it is essential to establish the culture you want so as not to have a culture vacuum. By 2004 Strauss was one group with a unique culture and a vision, poised for an exciting new beginning.

Intentional or not, all companies have a culture. Successful companies invest in developing a unique and positive culture. Conversely, unsuccessful companies struggle as their negative culture leads to dissention and becomes an obstacle to growth. I once worked with a small home-improvement company that had a toxic culture. It was a classic example of a total disconnect between the internal values and the external values, enabled by the business owner and the management team. The general manager tended to say one thing but then do something different. It was comical and sad as he stood in the front of the room one day addressing the sales team, clearly stating, "I do not lie." If he had bothered to look around the room, he would have noticed the expression on everyone's face: disbelief. Everyone knew he was lying about not lying. I even had said to him one time, "your actions are so loud, I can't hear your words." The lack of leadership throughout the organization resulted in constant chaos.

The owner and the general manager were both convinced that deception was the norm, which undermined any teamwork they hoped to achieve. The company purposely had devised a process that prevented communication among the sales team, the back office, and the production team. Imagine a company that prevents people from speaking to each other and helping each other with the management having convinced themselves that this is the right thing to do. The higher-ups at this home-improvement company talked about teamwork, but in practice there was no incentive for people to help each other. The owner and the general manager micromanaged every detail because they felt theyt could not trust anyone in the organization. The general manager's "I'm in charge," self-absorbed, know-it-all attitude trickled down to the handful of lower-level managers and promoted a toxic, dishonest environment.

The result was a revolving door of employees, most lasting less than six months. Any individual with intelligence and integrity figured out in a very short span of time that this company was troubled, so such people quickly exited. Unnecessary resources were continuously being spent hiring and training new employees on basic sales systems, instead of retaining smart, motivated employees and mentoring them to become consistent high sales performers. Management claimed that the rate of employee turnover was the industry norm, but other companies in the industry had good rates of employee retention.

Unfortunately, the deception also affected customers. There were rumors of forging customers' signatures, cashing customer rebate checks, and contractors billing for work they did not perform, all leading to dissatisfied customers. Most businesses take pride in providing superior products and services to delight their customers. Although this company did represent well-known premium products, the culture of deception and cheating delivered overpriced and subpar installations, resulting in disgruntled customers. As a result, they had poor reviews with frequent customer complaints and lawsuits.

The sad truth is that with a lot less effort, they could have developed a positive and supportive culture, resulting in positive teamwork and a great company. With a different culture and a different strategy, the company could have easily doubled their sales. This is a classic case of how not to do things. When the company values are dishonesty, distrust, cheating, and lying, it leads to a toxic culture, which results in a spiral of declining sales and eventual extinction. The company managers did not understand leadership, and because they were insecure with themselves, they surrounded themselves with people who would not challenge them, which had the result of making them feel secure in their own ineptitude. Good leaders are comfortable in their own skin and are not afraid to surround themselves with exceptional talent. Good leaders push everyone to new heights.

Companies frequently hire me as a strategy consultant. Before I engage in any strategy discussions, I spend a little time on company vision and culture. I like to start with making sure there are shared values and that those values are respected and lived throughout the company. It's not about posters on the walls but about actions. Do the company leaders walk the talk? If the answer is not obvious, we engage in an exercise identifying common values everyone can agree to. Many times I'm surprised how an executive team tries to lead a company without shared values. They look at all types of business indicators but forget that a unique company culture and shared values are the cornerstone of a successful company.

I hear a lot of negative comments about companies not being human, and some people have a perception that corporations are the enemy of people. Regardless if a company is small, maybe ten people, or large, made up of twenty thousand people, companies are still a collection of human beings whose behavior will be governed by the company culture and values. This is no different from a collection of individuals with their own character and values.

I was speaking with Pat Gelsinger, CEO of VMware, at an event. Pat is a Christian with a strong character and strong values that influence the way he leads his company. VMware is famous for its culture defined by EPIC2 values: execution, passion, integrity, customer, and community. I asked Pat the following question: "With more than twenty thousand employees across one hundred twenty countries, is it difficult to ensure EPIC2 is lived throughout your organization?"

Without hesitation Pat answered, "Not really. We make sure we all walk the talk. For example, just last week we had a sales meeting in China, and we did the usual partying that salespeople like to do. But we also used the time for everyone to volunteer on a local construction project to make sure we honored our value of giving back to the community." A company with a strong culture that is reinforced through continuous action in the organization will be healthy.

I also had the opportunity to speak with Lesley Hoare, who was leading talent development for VMware at the time. Lesley shared with me some of the programs they used, like a total culture immersion boot camp for new employees. They also required that each new manager attend in-person face-to-face training followed by additional online training, concluding with a feedback rating mechanism from colleagues or subordinates. The company made sure people throughout the organization bought into the company culture and lived it each day.

Dabo Swinney, the head coach of the Clemson football team, masterfully summarized, after a comeback win over the Buckeyes, what a winning culture is: "Unbelievable character and heart and a will to win. That's the one thing I told [my players]—[our opponents] can prepare for what we do but not for who we are. Our heart will win out in the end."

People often ask me for advice when looking for new opportunities. I suggest that before anyone even agrees to a job interview, they should do some research and find out the culture and values of the company. A great example is the small but quickly emerging company LifeAid. My daughter Nicole was one of their regional sales executives for several years before moving on to join Uber Freight. LifeAid's ten values are clearly stated on their website, so there should not be any confusion about what someone is signing up for. Just reading those values, it becomes clear what the company culture is and what an employee is expected to do.

With today's information technology, it takes only a small investment of your time to find out what a prospective employer's culture and values are. You may be surprised to learn that some companies do not pay attention to their culture or that their values are not well-defined. During your research, if you find that a company lacks a culture or that its values are opposed to yours,

66   TOM KERESZTI

don't even take the interview. I promise you that if you do join that company, it'll be only a matter of time before you unhappily leave for better opportunities.

In some cases you may find that your values and the company's values are not exactly aligned. That is okay, but if their values contradict yours, then that's a red flag. One last thing to check would be the company vision. If the company vision is missing, is unclear, or rubs you the wrong way, that is a yellow flag. But more on vision in the next chapter.

Good leaders develop their character through a strong identity founded on clear values. Great companies do the same through a unique company culture built on shared values.

I would encourage you to ask yourself a few questions:

- *Do I have a clear identity, and am I comfortable in my own skin?*

- *What are five values that identify me in all aspects of my life?*

- *Am I consistent in all areas of my life?*

- *What is my passion in life?*

- *What am I really good at?*

- *Do people view me as genuine? That is, do I walk the talk?*

4

KEY #2—WHAT IS YOUR VISION?

> The only thing worse than being blind is having sight but no vision.
> —*Helen Keller*

DO YOU HAVE A CLEAR PICTURE OF YOUR FUTURE?

The second rule in Stephen Covey's *The 7 Habits of Highly Effective People* is to start with the end in mind. If you don't know where you're going, any road will take you there. Now I want to clarify that depending on who you talk to, the terms *purpose, vision,* and *mission statement* are sometimes interchangeable. In my definition, vision captures the long-term future, and although the vision evolves over time, it does not abruptly change course.

I heard Dave Martin once refer to cathedral vision. It is a great analogy. Construction of the Cologne Cathedral commenced in 1248 and was finally completed in 1880—more than six hundred years in the making. The famous architect Antoni Gaudi laid plans for the Sagrada Família Basilica in Barcelona with a projected completion time of two hundred years. Imagine formulating a vision that you know will take two hundred years to complete, a plan that by design will outlive your legacy. Now that is a long-term and a courageous inspirational vision.

Some people have the unique ability to see and predict their future. I have always admired Arnold Schwarzenegger's story. As a young man growing up in Austria, Arnold was subjected to his father's career plans for him, but before Arnold was eighteen years old, he set a different vision for himself. He said he would become Mister Universe, then a movie star and eventually a millionaire. Now that is a clear road map, and clarity can help you plan to make your dreams a reality. Arnold later grew that vision to include politics. Our visions are never finished; instead, they evolve over time, like a journey that never ends.

Even when it looks like you have accomplished what you had originally set out to do, you must constantly evolve your vision and take it one step farther. Vision is about your long-term future, so do not confuse it with short-range plans or targets. It took Arnold a lifetime of hard work, sacrifice, and perseverance to realize his dreams of becoming Mister Universe, a movie star, and governor of California.

In his book The Infinite Game, Simon Sinek uses Kodak as an example of a company that lost their way and became a fraction of the great company it once was. Kodak was founded on a great vision but through leadership changes, market conditions and other factors, over time they lost their vision or as Simon Sinek phrases it, *"they lost their cause"*. Vision does not change, strategy changes, tactics change, but without keeping loyal to vision, companies are doomed for failure.

In the late 1980s, Colgate-Palmolive retained C. K. Prahalad to help refine the company's long-term vision. Colgate, a leading consumer goods marketing company, managed its business units by using a matrix of categories and geographies. I was working for Dr. Frank Morelli at the time, and he helped me secure a spot on the global strategy team. Our team's responsibility was to identify the long-term vision for the body care category of products. It was a great learning experience early on in my career; I learned about marketing, brand equity, category management, decision-making matrixes, and financial discipline.

There are some subtle moments of my life that are etched in my memory. On one particular day, I was attending a general meeting led by CK, who was teaching us the difference between vision, strategy, and activities. To illustrate the point, CK did not use a specific company as an example but instead focused on an industry. Now, mind you, this was around 1988. For an example, CK put up a transparency on the overhead showing how the telephone, television, and computer industries would merge over the next twenty years. Companies like AOL or Netscape that were early internet pioneers weren't viable until the early 1990s, and streaming first appeared in 1995. It wasn't until 2007, some twenty years later, that the iPhone was introduced. Today we can watch TV on our phones, make calls from our computers, and buy smart TVs that can surf the internet. Hardware technology is not the determining factor, but the software is, in the form of applications or media. Now that is more than a long-term strategy; that is a vision.

I would encourage each person to have a personal vision statement to serve as his or her moral compass. My personal vision statement evolved over the course of many years. Early on I recognized I was a leader and always found myself in leadership situations or positions. The vision statement that took me many years to evolve is simple and clear: "Man of God, leader of Men." This is the foundation of all my decisions. John Maxwell said that we make a few major decisions in our lives and manage the thousands of small decisions based on those few big ones. That is what a strong vision statement will do for you—help you manage the thousands of small decisions you have to make each day.

Several years ago, when I was division CEO for the Strauss Group, we held our annual company meeting in Bucharest, Romania. We invited our top corporate and local leadership team along with key marketing and sales managers, about two hundred people. Our general manager in Romania, Eli, arranged a remarkable venue for the evening reception, what was then known as the Ceauşescu Royal Palace. What a breathtaking building. Over the years, I've had the privilege of visiting many of Europe's famous palaces, like the Schönbrunn Palace in Vienna, the Palace of Versailles,

Windsor Castle, and the Dolmabaçhe Palace in Istanbul. With endless crystal chandeliers, marble columns, and gilded ceilings, Ceauşescu Royal Palace ranked up there with the best.

The setting was spectacular. Eli arranged a private tour of the palace and then had the grand ballroom reserved for our company dinner. I opened the evening by welcoming everyone, delivering a short message, and handing out awards for top performers, then we all enjoyed the great food, fine wine, and fantastic mood. I was invited to join a group of our younger executives, and we lit up the dance floor and kept the bar open till almost 2:00 a.m. We had a lot of fun. One of the marketing managers took a special liking to me. As the evening was coming to the end, we headed back to the hotel and said our goodbyes in the lobby. I remember the inviting look in her eyes; many would have fallen for the temptation. My home was more than a thousand miles away. Who would know?

It's times like these when my vision statement helps me in making what I call small decisions. If I were to accept the invitation, how would that honor my wife and family? How would I still be a "man of God"? How would I be a "leader of men" once I showed up for work the next morning with my colleagues knowing what had transpired the evening before? It was an easy decision. I thanked everyone for a fun night, gave out some hugs, and retired to my room. With a clear vision and a strong character, you will find it easy and straightforward to make the daily small decision to keep yourself on your chosen path.

> Good business leaders create a vision, articulate the vision, passionately own the vision, and relentlessly drive it to completion.
>
> —*Jack Welch*

Your vision must be simple, easy to follow, and consistent no matter the circumstance. I admire time-tested companies with leading brands. All great brands have one thing in common, a simple and inspiring vision or mission statement. If you examine the brand history of these great companies, you'll notice they haven't changed much in fifty-plus years and have evolved over time, for example, Coca-Cola's "We refresh the world," Nike's "We unleash human potential," and Microsoft's "We empower every person and organization to achieve more."

Notice the power of simplicity and the ease of understanding each vision statement. We can easily recognize a Coke bottle anywhere in the world. It looks very similar whether in the USA, Japan, Brazil, South Africa, or Saudi Arabia, regardless of the English, Hebrew, Arabic, Hanzi, or Ge'ez scripts, making the bottle easy to find. When you open that bottle, no matter where you are in the world, you have a guarantee that it will be refreshing. Coke stays true to its vision and is consistent everywhere. "We refresh the world" also means that you can find Coke anywhere you are. I'm sure that when we colonize Mars, Coke will be the first beverage there.

I would challenge you to think of yourself as a brand. As you begin to formulate your personal vision, make sure it is simple and easy to follow as it will help define who you are. If you are true to your vision, people will be able to recognize you in any environment no matter the circumstances. Your character and your vision will define everything you do and will help you ensure you are consistent in your actions regardless if you are at work, with your family, out with friends, or on vacation.

I must confess, I did not grasp this concept early on in my career. I acted very differently in a business setting as opposed to a private setting, and people noticed. People at work would always see me as proper, professional, and a little stiff with a touch of arrogance. I put on a professional face, keeping my distance from people. I was always open and friendly, an extrovert, easily warming up to people and having a few drinks after work, but never letting my guard down to form any true relationships at work. That was my professional face, all business.

On weekends I was a very different person. Footloose and fancy-free, I focused on enjoying life to its fullest with a different set of close friends. Each summer between 1980 to 1990, along with a group of friends, I would rent a house in the Hamptons (New York). From Memorial Day to Labor Day, I spent each weekend, and my vacation time, in a celebratory frenzy. Our typical weekend was to arrive by 10:00 Friday night, enter the Hamptons' party twilight zone, and check out 10:00 Sunday night for the trip home.

I could fill an entire book with just stories about the Hamptons, and maybe one day I will. Just to give you an idea, one of our favorite places was Ed's Bay Pub, one of the most unique establishments I've ever visited. Summer rentals were very common in the Hamptons, and each house came up with their own name. Ours was named the House of Ho. Ed set up a competition among the different houses where each house had to put on a lip-synch show. Our house won a trophy each year with skits from *The Wizard of Oz, Gypsy*, and many more. Many weekends we performed a lip-synch rock and roll medley show featuring the songs of Al Jolson, Jerry Lee Lewis, Buddy Holly, and Bob Seger. If Instagram or YouTube had been around in the 1980s, we would be famous now with millions of followers. The House of Ho had been around for many years before the reality show *Jersey Shore* became a huge hit.

One weekend I invited my colleagues John Sheridan and Joe Jeffs to our annual Christmas in July party, which we held every July 4th weekend. This particular year I had been asked to be the swill-meister, a job that resulted in everyone's at the party to feeling very happy given their indulgence in alcohol. I took this job very seriously and excelled at it. Around midnight, John and Joe pulled Kathy, my wife, aside with a look of great concern. One of them said, "There is something very wrong with Tom."

Kathy asked, "What do you mean?"

With all seriousness, John and Joe expressed that I had multiple personalities as they perceived me to be very different as a professional at work. Kathy assured them this was just the normal weekend version of me having fun.

I knew John and Joe well as I had spent about six months working with them on a project in Ohio. Each week, Monday through Friday, we worked, ate, and socialized together, but I always projected a professional image, even in a social setting. That evening they witnessed a different me, a partier in overdrive. I learned over the years that to form true relationships, I must be consistent wherever I am. Now that is not to say I should conduct myself the same way at work as I do on a Friday evening out on the town, but it does mean being authentic always.

Many of my colleagues were fun people, and once we got to know each other, I formed great relationships with them. In 1991, I had been assigned my first international assignment, and my boss and mentor Dr. Frank Morelli had arranged a farewell party for me at his house, inviting our colleagues and families. Somehow (thanks to my wife Kathy) a video recording of the *Wizard of Oz* skit performed by the House of Ho at Ed's Bay Pub made it to this party. Now if this had happened six years before, I would have been petrified before the video rolled. There I was onstage, starring as the lead munchkin, as my Colgate colleagues were watching the video. Everyone was laughing. It was a lot of fun. Instead of being embarrassed, I was embraced for my craziness and creativity. It turns out that in all walks of life, people love to have fun, and it is much easier to form relationships by having fun together.

> You have to leave the city of your comfort and go into the wilderness of your intuition. What you'll discover will be wonderful. What you'll discover is yourself.
> —*Alan Alda*

A good vision will steadily guide you, but strong intuition will help remove obstacles that arise along the way to reaching your goals. As I matured in my career and became CEO of the coffee division of the Strauss Group, I knew the value of forming close relationships with my teammates and their families. I also made sure we had plenty of fun along the way.

Federico was a friend and colleague at Benckiser, the previous company I'd worked for. I knew he was a great marketer. I got to know his wife Diana and their son Alberto. As I began to assemble my team, I thought of Federico first and asked if he would join my team. He said he'd be glad to. He became our VP of marketing.

I grew up in New York City. One meets a lot of people in New York. One of the things I learned was how to gauge people. To this day, I can spend an hour with someone and determine their main motives and discover if they are genuine or fake. I call it street smarts; John Maxwell calls it intuition. It was my intuition to hire Federico. We are all intuitive, especially in our comfort zone, our areas of strength. Leaders have great intuition as it allows them to see the future before others are able to. This arises from our strength to recognize patterns based on historical experience, to quickly analyze facts, to recognize trends, to piece it all together in anticipation of the future, and most importantly to take action.

As one of our fun trips, Federico arranged for a fabulous weekend in Verona for our leadership team and our spouses. Verona is a beautiful Northern Italian city not too far from the Alps. In true Italian form, Verona is rich in history, food, wine, and opera. We started our weekend with a great meal at Antica Bottega del Vino, visited Juliet's House, enjoyed a performance of *Carmen* in the colosseum, and finished our weekend off with a tour of the Allegrini winery. But the most memorable day started as Federico arranged lunch for us at the famous Locanda San Vigilio on the shores of Lake Garda.

Before lunch, we had time for a boat tour of the lake. Our captain was an older gentleman. He had displayed a picture of him piloting the boat with Winston Churchill on a similar tour of the lake. As we crossed the lake, enjoying the sunshine, the captain pointed out some of the gorgeous villas and told us stories and scandals of their past. Suddenly he looked up and simply said, "If we are going to get back for lunch, then we'd better get started now." The boat was relatively small, maybe seventeen feet, and in a matter of minutes the sky had turned dark with the water swelling. Suddenly we found ourselves in the middle of our version of *The Old Man and the Sea* with howling winds and swells of ten feet or higher. Cushions were flying off the deck, we were physically trying to hold onto the canvas covering, and one of the wives became sick. I was so concerned that I even called my daughters to let them know I loved them and missed them. To add to the excitement, the captain was blasting the "William Tell Overture" on his audio system. As I glanced toward the back of the boat, I saw Peter holding on for dear life with a huge ten-foot wake behind him and a silly grin on his face like a kid on a roller-coaster ride. Thanks to our captain, we safely made it back to San Vigilio. As we were calming our nerves with some prosecco, we saw a racing sailboat pass by with an unusual twenty people on it. The next day we read in the papers that the racing flotilla had lost eight boats in the storm; in total, twelve boats had sunk on the lake that day. This was a great example of how our captain had mastered the art of intuition. He recognized the cloud patterns as he had seen many storms quickly develop. He analyzed the facts, predicted the trends, and projected the outcome. His experience led him to make a quick decision that was not up for debate: we had to leave that moment if we were going to get back to the other side of the lake. Thanks to his intuition and decision, we safely made it back for a fabulous lunch.

It is never too late to establish a vision if you don't have one. It is also essential to recognize that as companies grow through acquisitions, their visions may evolve, so it is important to make sure that the sum of the parts still equals one uniting vision.

In 2001, I was asked to lead the international coffee division of the Strauss Group, as I've mentioned before. It was an ideal opportunity as the Strauss Group was in the process of establishing their identity after a major merger and multiple acquisitions. We worked on identifying a unique company culture as well as establishing our vision and values. As with all vision statements, we agreed that ours had to be simple, capturing the essence of who we were as an organization. It was to be our long-term road map, helping every major decision affecting our business, such as acquisitions and product launches. The Strauss vision statement became "Creating Wonders out of Basics." Now when you first read it, it sounds very simple, almost childish. But it had been Strauss's ability for three generations to take the most basic of raw materials, like milk, greens, vegetables, grain, cocoa, or coffee beans, and turn them into a moment of enjoyment of life. Imagine the wonderful feeling of biting into a cookie that tastes like the ones your grandmother used to make, or wrapping both your hands around a warm mug of coffee on a brisk morning, or gathering around the table with your family, sharing laughter while snacking on a communal bowl of baba ghanoush. These are the small daily wonders in our lives, things that create those warm and fuzzy feelings that lead us to conceive of "Creating Wonders out of Basics."

With a clear vision, we established a decision-making matrix to help us prioritize and to ensure that any new product or company acquisition would help us enhance our vision. We also merged our five company values into one sentence, stating, "We advance partnerships as a way to increase the scope and scale of our activity and create greater value for society." As my mentor once said, one is too small of a number to achieve greatness. Strauss fully embraced this principle and established joint ventures and acquisitions as a key building block in our growth strategy.

I will dedicate the next chapter to strategy, but I will say here that a clear vision helps construct a successful strategy. Without a clear vision, it is easy to end up with a collection of seemingly exciting projects that can take a company in very different directions. A clear vision will help a company to prioritize which projects or activities will better support its vision and to eliminate projects that do not contribute to the vision.

Colgate-Palmolive was a good example of this. In the 1960s and 1970s, one of the favorite terms on Wall Street was *acquisitions*. Many

Fortune 500 companies sustained growth by going on shopping sprees. Now there is nothing wrong with an acquisition growth strategy, but after more than ten years, and without a clear focus, Colgate found itself with a disconnected portfolio of companies. They were in the personal care business, in the cleaning business, in the food business, in the medical business, in the pet business, and in the crystal business, just to name a few. In the 1980s, I was part of the strategic team that shed most of those businesses because they did not fit the criteria of our new strategy as defined by our vision. Going forward, acquisitions remained an integral part of Colgate's growth strategy, but the acquisition candidates were first vetted to ensure they fit with the company vision. An example is the first major acquisition after we realigned our vision. Colgate acquired Mennen, a fast-growing deodorant company, which was a clear fit with our vision and body care strategy. Since that time Colgate has acquired many other companies, all aligned with their vision, building value for their consumers and shareholders.

One last thought about vision. In the last chapter I said that I feel strongly that there has to be a strong link between a person's values and the values of the company he or she works for. Equally important is that you understand and buy into the company vision. A company's vision should not contradict your personal vision. If the two are contradictory, I suggest that you not work at that company. If the company vision is confusing to you, or if you do not believe in it, do yourself a favor and move on. You will not be happy there, and it will be only a matter of time before you become frustrated and leave.

My daughter Alex does a good job at vetting what a company stands for before she agrees to work with them. She is an avid hiker, fitness instructor and has a love for photography. She has hiked Mount Whitney, Mount Shasta, Mount Hood, and the Half Dome in Yosemite, just to name a few. She is also a spin instructor and a yoga instructor who owns her adventure yoga company, Hike and Flow. Combining her three passions, she has built a great following on Instagram and Facebook, and over the last year many companies have reached out, asking her to promote their products by using those products and posting pictures. Before committing, Alex researches a company's culture, vision, values, and mission statement. Then she determines whether or not she will work with that specific company. She has been very selective and has turned down several revenue opportunities with companies whose vision or values she does not believe in. I encourage you to do the same. You will have a much easier time getting up each morning and looking yourself in the mirror and a much more gratifying experience at the end of each day.

If you do not have a vision statement, I would encourage you to ask yourself a few questions:

- *Do I have a vision for my life?*

- *Is my vision clear and easy to understand?*

- *Is my vision long term or just a short-term wish list of things I want?*

- *Do I use my vision as a foundation for major decision-making?*

5

KEY #3—IS YOUR STRATEGY
A GROWTH STRATEGY?

> You never know what results will come
> from your action. But if you do nothing,
> there will be no results.
>
> —*Mahatma Gandhi*

I have never met a successful person who is not constantly striving to grow. No one wants to become worse than they are today; they do not want to be poorer, be in worse health, or be more out of shape. I seek opportunities each day to grow and become a better person than I was yesterday. Every company I have ever worked for had a growth strategy. A healthy strategy is a growth strategy. But what separates a good strategy that will succeed from a bad strategy destined to fail?

Vision is fundamental to any strategy. Without a clear vision, developing a strategy is of no benefit. I had a Harley-Davidson for many years and loved riding it on the open roads. I met some people who became great friends and found camaraderie among motorcycle riders, especially Harley owners. In early 2005 when I moved to Northern California, I rode out to Alice's Restaurant on Skyline Drive in Woodside on a brisk sunny Saturday morning. A small wood cabin nestled beneath some giant redwoods, Alice's is positioned to provide access to the most glamorous country roads in the San Francisco Bay Area. It is a famous spot where motorcycle riders, otherwise known as weekend warriors, gather and ride the spectacular country roads of the Pacific coast with its redwoods.

Being new to California and not knowing anyone, I parked my bike and grabbed a beer, sitting down to see what life would bring my way. I overheard two guys, Dave and Eleu, talking about riding to Santa Cruz for a clam chowder cook-off, so I introduced myself and asked if I could join them and ride with them. The three of us rode our shining Harleys along the sunny coastal road US 1 to Santa Cruz to enjoy the boardwalk festivities. As the clam chowder cook-off was winding down, Dave and Eleu made it their personal mission to become the best tour guides anyone could wish for. They took me on several more stops before sundown. As we pulled up to the Black Watch in Los Gatos, they each called their girlfriends and apologized for having to cancel on dinner plans that evening, saying they had to show me around. That started a friendship that is still strong today.

We have gone on hundreds of rides together and have enjoyed an endless number of fun trips. Most important, we have been there for each other in times of need. My wife Kathy always made fun of me when I went out riding with Dave, Eleu, and other friends. When Kathy would ask me where we were going, I never had a clear answer. I was not being difficult. My friends and I would meet in the morning and decide if we were going to travel north, south along the coast, or inland. We never had a plan. The day was not about a goal or destination; we were just enjoying the ride and the fellowship, going wherever the road took us.

I loved the Saturdays we went out riding together, but if I had been living my life the same way, without direction, then I would have been a total failure. It is one thing to ride and discover the countryside, take in nature's beauty, make friends, and stumble upon a local place to share a great meal. See, activity is not necessarily an accomplishment. To grow as an individual or as an organization, one must have an intentional growth strategy and plan. You can only grow intentionally; growth cannot happen by accident.

No one ever became a success by accident, so you must be intentional about growing. We are all better at some things than others. I suggest you focus growing in your strength zone. Some of us are more analytical, others are more creative, others are great teachers, and still others have better people skills. We are all created equal, but we are wired very different to excel in the areas where we are strong. When my daughter Nicole was still very young, I always took the opportunity to mentor her in negotiation. We were always together on weekend outings and vacations, and she watched me negotiate with people all the time in all kinds of environments.

One year when Nicole was about ten years old, we were in Italy walking around. My wife Kathy is like a magnet for bazaars, and sure enough we stumbled on a bunch of street vendors and began browsing through dozens of kiosks, mostly offering leather stuff. We always came home from any vacation with more stuff than we'd originally packed for the trip. On display in one of the kiosks was a bunch of leather purses. One small colorful purse caught Nicole's eye. She turned to me and said, "Dad, I really like this. Can I have it?"

I sensed a teaching moment. We kept walking until we were well away from the kiosk and the vendor could no longer see us. Although the purse was priced much higher, I gave Nicole five thousand lira and encouraged her that she could buy it for that much. I stood about three kiosks away, keeping an eye on her as she negotiated with the vendor for almost twenty minutes. She was relentless and would not give up charming the vendor with her cuteness and persistence. In the end she broke him down. Beaming, with a huge smile, she walked away with her new purse.

Nicole always had great people skills and is now flourishing in sales, having started with Red Bull, then moving on to Vita Coco and LifeAid, and most recently working for Uber Freight. She has leveraged her strength; being able to easily connect with people and to influence them has propelled her into a great sales career. She started as a sales rep, then became a regional manager, then a business development manager, and then a territory manager. Now she manages multimillion-dollar accounts. With each promotion, she continues to grow in her strength, leading and influencing people.

My other daughter Alex has very different strengths. She is extremely creative and has built up a solid following on Instagram. She has a passion for mountain climbing, she has a creative eye for photography, and she is a physical fitness guru. As she challenges herself with intense hikes like summiting Mount Whitney in a day, she takes breathtaking photographs. She is now creating a documentary, *Small Towns to Summits*, climbing the six highest peaks in the western United States. Her Instagram following continues to grow, and it is starting to amount to regular income. Alex is able to influence others through her stories accompanied by her photography and some breathtaking natural settings for her photographs. She also continues to grow by challenging herself to bigger hikes, with Kilimanjaro on her radar.

Both Nicole and Alex are driven, but their success is a function of having developed their own individual strengths. Alex does not have the people connection skills like Nicole, and Nicole does not have the creative gifts of Alex. Simple logic will tell you Nicole should work on being more creative and Alex should work on her people skills to make them each a more rounded individual. There is some truth to that, but there are limits to how much you can improve in an area that is not your strength. Michael Jordan is a naturally gifted athlete who has honed his basketball skills over a lifetime. For a short stint, he tried baseball and did poorly in the minors. His strength is basketball, not baseball, so that is where he invested his efforts. Each person is much better served by finding their strength then investing and growing in that area.

Intentional growth is a result of a well-thought-out strategy, founded on researched facts, and a plan that is realistic and executable. You may have heard the famous story of two expedition teams trying to reach the South Pole for the first time in 1911. One team was led by a Norwegian explorer, Roald Amundsen, while the other team was led by a British explorer, Robert Scott. Amundsen's team reached the Pole thirty-four days before the other team, and Scott's team never made it back, freezing to death on the return journey.

Both teams had the same goal; however, they had different strategies, one of which was successful and the other of which end in death. Amundsen had decided not to wear the heavy wool clothing worn on earlier attempts to reach the South Pole. Instead he elected to use furred skins like those worn by Eskimos. He also chose using skis and dog sleds for transportation, similar to what the Native Eskimos used. Amundsen and his men created supply depots along a line directly south to the Pole. He also planned to kill some of his dogs on the way to use them as a source of fresh meat.

Scott, on the other hand, had decided on a mixed transport strategy, relying on contributions from dogs, motorized sledges, and ponies. Progress was slower than expected because the motorized sledges did not hold up in arctic temperatures and the ponies' performance was adversely affected as Scott's team had left their snowshoes behind. On December 14, 1911, Amundsen's team of five, with sixteen dogs, arrived at the South Pole. They arrived thirty-four days before Scott's group, and then they made their way off the continent and on to Hobart, Australia, where Amundsen publicly announced his success.

Tragically, as previously stated, Scott's team froze to death and never made it back from their journey. Amundsen's expedition benefited from his careful preparation, good equipment, appropriate clothing, a simple primary task, an understanding of dogs and their handling, and the effective use of skis. In contrast to the misfortunes of Scott's team, Amundsen's trek proved relatively smooth and uneventful. In Amundsen's own words: "I may say that this is the greatest factor, the way in which the expedition is equipped, the way in which every difficulty is foreseen and precautions are taken for meeting or avoiding it. Victory awaits him who has everything in order—luck, people call it. Defeat is certain for him who has neglected to take the necessary precautions in time; this is called bad luck."

To help develop a growth plan, it is necessary to interpret the past. We must learn from the past to see how we must do things differently in the future. Experience is only helpful if we learn from it; otherwise it is just stuff that happens to us. I personally learned one very important growth lesson the hard way. John Maxwell writes in *The 21 Irrefutable Laws of Leadership* about the law of the lid. He says each individual has a leadership lid defining how good of a leader he or she is at any one time. Each person can raise that lid by investing in himself and growing as a leader, but the other reality is that a person will never follow another leader whose leadership lid is rated lower than his own. That was my shortcoming early on in my career. I needed to realize that if I was to grow as a leader,

I needed to have patience when my boss had a lower perceived leadership lid than I.

As I advanced in my career, I would have a new boss about every three years as I took on new challenges. I reported to people I highly admired and respected, like Dr. Frank Morelli. I also had bosses whom I respected much less, for example, Bob. Bob was a nice guy, so there was no personal conflict, but after about six months, I could not understand why I was reporting to him instead of the other way around. The relationship was not a healthy one as I challenged many of Bob's decisions. Eventually I was promoted to a different department. This same scenario played out several times with other managers in my early career, and each time I was promoted soon enough without incident.

When Colgate-Palmolive first promoted me to an expatriate assignment, the first three years were a honeymoon. As Colgate-Palmolive Hungary's head of operations, I found it to be very exciting starting up a new company, establishing an infrastructure, building brands, launching new products, and acquiring a local company. Patrick was my boss initially, but because of an unfortunate series of personal problems, he left the company. I had worked hard for three years building the company and had left my handprint on most of the accomplishments. I was well-liked by all the employees, so naturally I thought I would be promoted to general manager. Well, that did not happen.

Colgate-Palmolive, like many multinationals, had a succession plan, and Ken Kodem from Denmark, a sales specialist, was chosen as the GM. Although disappointed, I sucked it up and continued to lead all operations, including finance. Over time, I developed respect for Ken's sales knowledge, but I had little respect for his leadership. His people skills were desperately lacking; he was a highly introverted individual who was very distant and rubbed most people the wrong way.

Some moments are etched in the memory forever. I had such a moment in 1995. We were planning our annual company meeting, and Ken had asked me to do a presentation on operations. We did not compare notes. It is important to know that I spoke fluent Hungarian, whereas Ken did not. Ken started the meeting with his presentation. Frankly, his story did not connect well with the audience and did nothing to motivate the people in attendance. I was up after Ken, and I knocked it out of the park with a presentation on shareholder value. My speech was engaging, and I connected with the people, receiving a standing ovation. I saw the look on Ken's face and knew right away that something was very wrong. Ken's leadership lid was noticeably below mine. At that moment he had come to understand that the team would follow me before they would follow him. Like many people, Ken was insecure about his position and could not embrace other strong leaders around him. About six months after that presentation, Ken relieved me of my duties without cause.

There are two types of leaders, strong leaders who want to develop future leaders and seek out individuals with high leadership potential, and insecure leaders who feel threatened by other leaders and seek to have followers. Ken was the second type. Oddly

enough, Colgate parted with him the next year for making a mess
of things. The lesson for me was obvious: if I was going to grow as
an individual and as a leader, I had to change my mindset about
authority. I learned that regardless of what I thought about the
individual I reported to, I needed to respect the office and position he
or she held. If I exceeded expectations with my own achievements,
I would be promoted and therefore would not be stuck long term
reporting to an individual who had a lower leadership lid than I.

Creating a growth strategy and navigating a successful path
requires clear direction and a predictable future based on an
accurate interpretation of the past. Businesses create a picture
of the future by developing a strategic plan or business plan.
Most plans look three years into the future and chart the course.
The plan is reviewed each year and adjusted based on results,
outside parameters, competition, and other circumstances. Many
companies issue top-down targets of sales and profit growth,
leaving it to their staff to come up with the details. I understand
the need for top-down targets in large organizations, but without
substance these targets, which always result in empty promises, are
guaranteed to fail.

I remember sitting in strategy business reviews hearing comments
like "We will grow sales by 25 percent" or "We will increase profits
by 20 percent," but those statements are all measurements, not
plans. A P&L or a balance sheet is simply a tool to measure how
well a business is performing; it is not the plan itself.

Reckitt Benckiser was great at ensuring strategic plans had substance. They were scrutinized during the planning review process by peers and bosses alike. I remember the first strategic planning process shortly after I was appointed as GM for Benckiser's Eastern European subsidiary. My team and I developed a three-year growth plan in late August that was probably 80 percent complete, but we knew it would be refined. At one point we met with our sister subsidiary companies in the region and did a dry run, providing feedback on each other's plans. My team quickly learned we needed more substance in our product launches and distribution-building activities to increase the confidence of others in their success. In September, we met with Bart Becht, our CEO, along with our sister subsidiaries, to present our revised strategic budget. Bart had some tough questions and good suggestions, but ultimately he approved our budget consisting of real activities supported by soundly researched assumptions. By October we had final approval, and in November we started implementing our plan to get an early start on the new year. It was a model that I successfully adopted for my future business planning.

> Unless you try to do something beyond what you have already mastered, you will never grow.
> —*Ralph Waldo Emerson*

The number one is too small a number to achieve greatness. It is much easier to grow with others than alone. If you look at most successful companies, you will see that their strategic growth plans usually include internal organic growth from new customer and new products, but they also include acquisitions or joint ventures.

In 2001, when I joined the Strauss Group, in addition to a new vision, we also formulated a new growth strategy. The coffee industry was very spread out in emerging countries. In western Europe and the USA, the consolidation was complete, but in eastern Europe and Latin America, the local landscape showed multiple local coffee roasters in each country. A key part of our growth strategy was to consolidate in the major coffee-consuming markets of eastern Europe and Brazil. In three years, we acquired five coffee companies in Brazil, Serbia, and Poland to boost our presence in those regions. But how we achieved success is very interesting.

A good strategy is to understand how to leverage your strengths. In Strauss's case, we were able to leverage our weakness and turn it into an advantage. It was always the same multinational players, Kraft and Sara Lee, wooing the local businesses they wished to acquire. When they negotiated with the owners of these local companies, the discussions always went something like this: "We love the company you built, and we value your contribution, but we want to buy 100 percent of your company, and if that's not possible, we must start by purchasing 51 percent and have in place a clear road map to get to 100 percent in five years or less." In other words, the family members who had built the company lost control from day one. The multinational would send in its management team and give some token position to the family members.

Strauss had a different approach. First, we realized that we did not have a deep bench of C-suite executives ready to take over and run a local company. However, we did have an abundance of excellent finance guys. We recognized that these local roasters individually had built their businesses over the course of time. In some case, the earlier generations of their family built the company. They took pride in their ownership, hard work, and business success. When we were negotiating with them, our approach was to make sure they would have a meaningful influence on the business going forward. Strauss offered to buy only 50 percent, capturing the essence of a pure joint venture, with no pressure to increase our share over a predefined period of time. We asked the local ownership to stay on in key leadership positions like general management or sales, but we did mandate that our Strauss finance person be the local CFO to ensure we had strong control of the balance sheet, investments, and expenditures. We recognized the owners' business-building skills and wanted them to continue, but we kept a close eye on the kitty.

The reality was that by not forcing the issue, most local owners sold us the majority of their businesses a few years later anyway. This same growth strategy also led us to the realization that we could team up with a major global coffee company on a large scale. In addition to our local activities, we met with several global coffee companies to explore collaborations, even acquisitions.

In 2002, we teamed up with Lavazza, the largest and most recognized Italian coffee roaster. The Strauss and Lavazza families signed a memorandum of understanding agreeing Strauss would sell, market, and distribute Lavazza in the emerging markets of

eastern Europe and Latin America. Every time we were about
to finalize a merger or acquisition, officers from both companies
would meet to sign the legal documents. Ofra Strauss, who had
a pen fetish, would always purchase a fancy unique fountain pen
for all members of both company teams to commemorate the
event. For the Lavazza signing, she went all out and gave us each a
memorable Monteverde. I still have mine today. It is a gorgeous pen
with a gold tip and a swirled green marble body presented in a hard
display case. It was a lot of fun teaming up with others to realize
our growth plan. Together we can always achieve more than we can
individually, by ourselves.

Abundance mindset over a zero sum game will always lead to a
successful growth strategy. Are you a pelican or a seagull? Kathy
and I have been blessed to live on the beach for the last few years.
Nicole, our daughter, came to visit us recently and informed us that
the ocean is exactly ninety-two steps from our back door. I often
sit on my balcony to enjoy the most beautiful sunsets, and I am
disciplining myself for a quiet walk on the beach several times per
week. I was walking one morning and noticed a flock of pelicans
near the surf. As a team, they were all circling, scouting the water,
one by one diving out of the air into the water. There must have
been a school of fish running, and the pelicans were setting up for
an enjoyable sushi lunch.

As I watched the pelicans, I noticed that they were relentless in
their circling, diving, flying back up, circling, and diving again.
They drifted downstream with the school of fish, which migrate
south. I witnessed their impeccable teamwork and work ethic.

Occasionally I would see a pelican emerge from the water with a fish in its mouth—and that is when I noticed all the seagulls. While the pelicans were working hard diving into the ocean, the seagulls were just circling and watching. As soon as a pelican emerged from the water with a catch, the seagulls would invade its space, trying to get a share of the meal. Watching this reminded me of the old marketing saying "There are riches in niches."

Is your growth strategy based on creating new markets, introducing new products, and exploring new customer needs, or are you simply battling in the trenches, trying to gain share in an existing, established market? If you are a pelican, you will focus your energy on creating value through opportunities and building new markets. If you are a seagull, you will be competing in a zero-sum game, where your gain is someone else's loss and vice versa. By creating new markets, everyone wins, and it is no longer a zero-sum game. Think of Red Bull creating a new niche. How about Amazon or Facebook? They all created those new markets then dominated them as their companies grew. A healthy growth strategy never competes in a zero-sum game; it always creates new opportunities for growth.

Just because everyone is doing it does not make it smart or right. There are many copycat companies and copycat products that jump on the bandwagon and make the same mistakes with their similar approaches. They join in with the latest fad without thinking through the business model and, in fact, veering from their strategy, altering their direction, which makes it impossible to be in the moment. I am not talking about start-ups but about mature companies making costly mistakes.

My wife Kathy is the shopper in our family. When we were living in England, she once convinced me to go to downtown London on Boxing Day. I was told that it was the only day in London when there were sales. With our two young daughters, we dragged my friend Shane, who was visiting us at the time, along. I think the entire population of London was squeezed into about ten square blocks. It was a madhouse as we tried to navigate the sidewalk on Regent Street with thousands of people. It was similar to a rock concert, elbow to elbow, people bouncing off each other. As we walked from store to store, I even got caught up in the hype and purchased a pair of Bally shoes "on sale" just to join in the fad. My shoes ended up being half a size too small, and I only wore them a handful of times. Talk about getting caught up in the moment and making a mistake. Do not get caught up in the hype. If it fits your strategic growth model, then go for it, but do not alter your course just because everyone else is doing it.

One of my favorite books is John Maxwell's *The 21 Irrefutable Laws of Leadership*. In it he talks about the law of momentum; like a locomotive, life, once it gains momentum, is difficult to stop. If your plans are working, then fuel the fire and keep the momentum going. In 1984 a group of us took a ski trip to Austria. In those days the US dollar was at its height, and our small budget took us a long way in Innsbruck using Austrian schillings. One evening, we all agreed to have some fun and take a bus ride over to visit an Italian casino.

During the ride, my friend Shane, who had never been to a casino, kept joking about letting it ride. Once we got there, we saw that the venue was a small European casino with a handful of tables. We all sat down to play blackjack. The minimum bet was equivalent to about $2.50. While most of us both won and lost a few hands, somehow Shane was able to tie or beat the house with each hand. Each time he just left the winnings on the table and repeated his famous phrase, "Let it ride."

Shane's winnings were visibly starting to pile up, until the dealer informed him, "Sir, you have reached the house limit." Shane, without hesitation, waved his arm and, with a raised voice, said, "Raise the limit." The dealer turned to the pit boss, who nodded in agreement to raise the limit. As luck would have it, Shane pulled blackjack on that last hand. In astonishment we all broke out in celebration, not knowing how much money he had just won. It turned out to be the equivalent of only $800, but it more than paid for his airfare and his hotels for the trip. Once he'd won, Shane cashed out and called it the evening. Now I do not condone gambling, but that was the best example of the law of momentum I've ever witnessed. If you are winning in life, do not take your foot of the gas pedal; keep going.

How does strategy differ from tactics? Strategy is preparation you do to make tomorrow better. Strategy is what you will do, and tactics involves the solid execution, the implementation of your strategy. Let us take for example the topic of time management. First, whoever tells you that such a thing exists is not telling you the truth. No one can manage time; we are all granted the same twenty-four hours in a day. It is what we do with those twenty-four hours that makes the difference. It is priority management that counts.

To execute your strategy, set the right priorities then divide them into four quadrants. Keep in mind that activity is not necessarily an accomplishment. First recognize the tasks that are urgent and important; second, those that are not urgent but are important; third, those that are urgent but not important; and finally, those that are not important and are not urgent. We usually do not have much choice in whether or not to address those tasks that are urgent and important. We will probably spend 40 percent of our resources on these tasks. The second set of tasks is crucial as many of us tend to put off tasks that are important but not urgent until one day they do become urgent. If we can spend at least 30 percent of our resources on these tasks, we will help achieve our growth objectives. For example, writing *C Suite and Beyond* was always important but never urgent.

It is equally important to systematically reduce the resources dedicated to tasks that are urgent but not important. This is difficult as we must recognize that certain tasks may be urgent and important to others but not necessarily important to our growth. When you analyze existing priorities, you will probably find that urgent tasks, important or not, is where you are spending 80% of your time. The best place to free up time for tasks that are important but not urgent is to eliminate tasks that are urgent but not important. If we can limit these tasks to consuming less than 25 percent of our resources, we will be well on our way to success.

And last, we should spend no more than 5 percent of our resources on tasks that are not urgent and not important.

On a macro level, my career was always high priority, consuming a significant amount of my time. I was the wage earner creating a comfortable life for my family. My job became important and urgent as I dedicated most of my daily schedule to traveling for business, sometimes for days at a time, or going to my office for extended hours. In 2003, I recall collecting over three hundred thousand miles on British Airways alone and a bunch more on Lufthansa. My typical week consisted of boarding a plane early Monday morning and returning Friday evening. Each month, I even had to spend a weekend in Israel in board meetings. During a three-year stretch, on average I spent three weekends per month at home, just a grueling and unsustainable schedule. That was about the worst it got, but at the time I had prioritized work as urgent and important.

I also knew that spending time with my family was important, but as a priority it always played second fiddle to my work schedule. We always took great family vacations, and on weekends I would help with sports teams, never mind supporting our kids' youth programs, but if I measure the time invested throughout years, I see it was below 20 percent. I still recall the discussion with Nicole at the age of sixteen when she said, "Dad, I haven't seen you half my life." Ouch, that one sentence hurt, finally hitting home that I had my priorities out of whack. Moving forward, I refocused my priorities and reserved a lot more time for my kids and family.

Although it may not have seemed urgent, I made sure to focus on what was important.

Set your priorities right. Just because something is not pressing doesn't necessarily mean it isn't very important. On the flip side to that, some things may seem urgent, but in reality they are not important. One last idea I learned from one of my mentors is to be proactive in managing your calendar and each day to focus your energy on the most important activity. I know I am my best between 8:00 a.m. and 2:00 p.m. The longer the day goes on, the less focused I become. I schedule my important meetings during these times and leave less important meetings for the late afternoon or early evening. I also make sure I block out time to prepare for those important meetings so I can be at my best.

The best thing about a crisis is that it forces you to examine your priorities. When a crisis hits, you learn very quickly how to prioritize between what is essential and what is just nice to have. During my expatriate career, we moved to a different country about every three years. Each time we would hire a local moving company, and they would send in a crew to pack up everything in the house. In every country we hired a different company, each with its own branded moving boxes. One of our moves, after the crew had finished packing, they began to load up the moving container. They found some boxes in the storage room, and as they were loading them on the truck, I recognized a different branded box from a moving company from several years ago, two moves ago. The box was never opened and just sat in storage for years. We had no idea of its contents.

Clearly whatever was in the box was not urgent and not important. If it were, we would have been looking for it a long time ago. We had lived without whatever was inside it for many years, so why did we even have it? This is a good analogy for many of the things we do each day, mostly out of habit, that do not add value to us or our businesses. A crisis will help set our priorities and make us shed those unimportant things. So what is your box sitting in your attic? Do not wait for a crisis; set you priorities and let it go.

> There will be today, perhaps some, who ridicule my predictions about the future of airplanes. Those who live, will see.
> —*Alberto Santos-Dumont*

The most challenging bridge in human history is the bridge between knowing and doing. Knowing is your strategy, and doing is the execution of your strategy. I had a lot of fun being Benckiser's general manager in the 1990s. First, I was living in Prague, one of the most enchanting cities in the world. Second, we were busy launching new products and developing new brands in a market ripe and hungry for change. All the Eastern European countries would meet together with Bart Becht, our CEO, for our annual regional strategic planning meeting. Each country presented their strategy, and we all received great input from our peers and superiors. Together with Bart, we would all meet for our quarterly business review to measure the progress we'd made on our plans.

Each time we found that some of the countries were not executing and were falling short, while others were even exceeding their plans.

We all knew what we had agreed and what we had to do, but some countries just would not do it. They never bridged the gap between knowing and doing. It was a consistent picture. Some countries like Russia consistently came up short on execution, while my subsidiary and Turkey always beat our plans. Caner Tunaman, the Turkish general manager, became a good friend over the years. He was a strong leader and great at executing plans. Russia was led by Janus, who was an ineffective leader who could not execute the simplest of plans. After a short time, he was replaced by a new general manager.

A great strategy without implementation is worthless. To have a winning strategy, you need a strong leader and a strong team to implement the details effectively.

Fleet Admiral William Halsey, during World War II, said, "Strike first, strike hard, and show no mercy." To execute your strategy, you need to act. While an expatriate executive, and in each country we moved to, I established a triangle focused on the family. Work was always a given being it was the reason we had moved to the country in the first place. The three legs of the triangle were our home, our place of worship, and our daughters' school. We always tried to find a home within a reasonable commute to the school to make sure Kathy and the girls were not constantly driving all over the place. I learned the hard way with my first overseas assignment that you cannot ignore your family's needs and focus only on the business challenges. I also learned it is essential that your spouse oversee the housing situation. Housing in Eastern Europe in the early 1990s was challenging.

When we first moved to Budapest, housing was scarce. Families living in temporary housing for six months was not uncommon. Whenever a listing would come on the market, about a dozen spouses would get in their cars and race to the property, each with a briefcase full of cash for a deposit. It was definitely a supplier's market, and apparently anything was feasible. My boss's wife Diana finally found a house. While waiting for her belongings in transit to be moved, she was attending an International Women's Club luncheon. The women at the table were showing off and exchanging stories as expatriate spouses love to do. Diana proudly boasted about this great house she had just landed on Szerena Street. Another woman at the table replied, "That is fantastic. Me too. We'll be neighbors."

"What number is your house?"

"Number fifty-five."

"Say what? That is my house," said the other.

Welcome to the wild and unpredictable Eastern Europe right after the collapse of the iron curtain. The owner had taken two deposits and signed lease contracts with both parties. In the end, there proved to be some legal avenue to take. Our company lawyers prevailed simply because Diana's contract had been signed a few days before the second contract and at a higher price. All is fair in war, but the person with the best lawyer usually wins.

> Do not be embarrassed by your failures.
> Learn from them and start again.
> —*Richard Branson*

To succeed, we have to fail many times. We often hear people say bravely, sometimes quoting others, that failure is part of learning and growing, or that it is not now many times you are knocked down that counts but how many times you get up. Companies even create cultures and compensation structures that do not punish failure but, rather, reward initiative. But let's face it, none of us likes to fail, and we are all petrified of what happens to us when we fail. Inspirational coach Aileen Gibb suggests that if we simply recognize that we will fail, we will gain clarity on the consequences of failure.

Most people overexaggerate what happens when they fail in a dramatic fashion, but in reality, our lives go on after a failure and, in most cases, actually improve. How do you turn adversity into an advantage? By reflecting. If you learn from your experiences, then your life will become better. I've had multiple failures, many small, a handful more significant, but I always learn from them.

My first life-changing failure was when my employment with Colgate was terminated. After fifteen years of being a star and being promoted about every three years, I was devastated to be out of a job. I was ashamed, lost, as if my whole identity had been wrapped up in my work. The first revelation came a few weeks after it all sank in, when I realized that my job was not who I was but was only one of the things I did. I was a husband, a father, a son, a church leader, and I also worked.

Soon enough headhunters were calling and interviews were happening, and within three months I had a great job offer at a great company—a higher-level position with more money. We moved into a bigger house and got a dog, and the girls were even happier.

Failure taught me two lessons. First I learned that my job did not define me, and second I learned how to become a free agent in the employment pool. I learned how to define and market myself as a brand, and I launched my expat career. Had it not been for failure and losing my job, I probably never would have become CEO and my family would not have gotten the opportunity to live in so many countries. So, when you fail, learn from the experience, move on, and continue to grow.

> Creative people are curious, flexible, persistent, and independent, with a tremendous spirit of adventure and a love of play.
> —*Henri Matisse*

Creative teams always incubate growth. For most companies that market and sell products, their strategy is led by their marketing teams. That is not to say other departments are not important. Finance must sign off on affordability, manufacturing has to make the product, and sales has to sell it, but creativity will always lead innovation. Every multinational company I have worked for was led by creative marketing people. I had great jobs early on in my career, but it was only once I had developed my marketing skills that I was given the opportunity to lead a company as a general manager and CEO.

In the 1980s, I shared a summer rental for ten years in the Hamptons with some of the craziest creative guys. One of my favorite stories is of when we all agreed to take a week's vacation together. After a great weekend, we were all at the house. Our friend John was about to drive his girlfriend home on Sunday afternoon, intending to return that evening to kick off our bachelor vacation. We decided to leave him a note on the kitchen counter and let him know where we would be. Creativity kicked into action and we hatched a plan to send John on a quest whereby he would receive instructions at each stop, eventually leading him to meet up with us. We went to several bars and explained the task to the bartenders, and they all agreed to play along. We paid for John's drinks in advance and asked each bartender to serve him the drink then give him an envelope revealing the specific instructions for John's next step. John, upon receiving his first instruction, assumed the role, dressing the part as Sherlock Holmes, and played along.

His first instruction was to walk up to the first bartender and say, "Hi, I'm Rommel, the Desert Fox. I've been wandering through the hot desert sand all day, and I'm thirsty. Do you have something for me?" At the first bar, the bartender gladly handed him a cocktail, along with an envelope with his next clue inside. His next instruction was to go to a different place and say to the bartender, "Hi, I'm Ponce de León. I've been searching for the fountain of youth, and I'm very thirsty. Do you have something for me?" Can you imagine the faces of the patrons in each establishment as this played out? The last instruction was "We are at the movies with Lee Marvin, Jane Fonda, and Nat King Cole." It was one of our favorite spots, a bar on the beach called Cat Ballou. John finally found us a few hours later, overjoyed with the experience. Most people would just have left simple instructions for John to meet them at Cat Ballou, but why waste a creative opportunity?

Creativity is not limited to conference rooms; be creative in all areas of life. You will have a lot more fun.

> I can't change the direction of the wind, but I can adjust my sails to always reach my destination.
> —*Jimmy Dean*

One of the buzzwords in start-up businesses is *pivot*. If your plan is not exactly working, then you should pivot and change direction. Well within reason. Vision should not change as it is the overarching picture, but it is okay to change strategy or tactics and pivot along the way to reaching your goal. I could say that my career has been full of pivots. Statistics show that people of my generation change careers 2.3 times in their lifetimes. Millennials pivot a lot more than that.

Over my career, I have pivoted from engineering, to IT, to finance, to sales, to marketing, to GM, and to CEO. After that I pivoted again, from corporate life to starting my own business. Now I am a coach and consultant working with companies and leadership teams, giving back and sharing my lifetime of learning, adding value to others. My most recent pivot was to write *C Suite and Beyond*, and my plan is to write many more books. Regardless of how many pivots I've taken in almost forty years, my vision has been steadfast— man of God, leader of men. Do not compromise your vision, but be flexible and pivot as markets change and life changes make it necessary for you to do so. To reach your destiny, adopt change, move forward, adopt change, move forward, and repeat as necessary.

Sometimes innovation or dramatic events force us to pivot. The rise of the internet forced many companies to pivot and reinvent themselves. Companies that stood still in this regard vanished. This also gave new companies like Amazon opportunities to flourish. Smartphones and apps changed the way we interact, allowing us to gain instantaneous information and make decisions. The events of 9/11 altered our security, our freedom, and the travel industry. The COVID-19 pandemic was a shock to our health-care industry with a shortage of medical devices, more global information sharing, and changes to the way FDA granted approval for certain medications or procedures. Social distancing, quarantine, and lockdown made us find new solutions. I had often thought about holding webinar workshops, but every time I found an excuse why I could not do it. The COVID-19 crisis forced me to pivot and to kick off my online workshops and a podcast. Dramatic events ensure that we never remain the same. A global crisis, for example, eliminates the status quo. But we must find a way to turn adversity into an advantage. If we do not pivot, reinvent ourselves, and find a new way, then we will become extinct.

Ask yourself some honest questions:

- *Do you have a growth plan? If so, how are you executing that plan?*

- *Is your strategic growth aligned with your vision?*

- *Are you growing, or could you grow faster through innovation and creativity?*

- *Have you prioritized your time and investments to support your growth plan?*

- *Are you creating new opportunities or just nurturing old ones?*

- *Are you teaming up with others to help yourself grow?*

- *Are you comfortable or open and ready to change?*

6

KEY #4—WHO IS ON YOUR TEAM?

> Incredible things in the business world are never made by a single person, but by a team.
>
> —*Steve Jobs*

W ho is in your inner circle? One is too small of a number to achieve greatness, and as humans we were not designed to be alone; rather, we work best in teams. The important question is, whom do we surround ourselves with, that is, who is on your team? Are the people in your inner circle there to help you reach new heights, or are they there to limit your achievements?

I admit I do not really understand today's social media. My kids are impressed with how many likes, how many friends, or how many followers they have and are disappointed if their followers do not number in the thousands. Although I also have thousands of followers on LinkedIn and Facebook, I can count the number of friends I have on one hand. True, trusted friends are few. My friend Shane is always on top of my friends list.

I met Shane in freshman year of high school, and we remained close until he passed away a few years ago. He was a confidant and, as they say, my brother from another mother. I discussed with him all major decisions in my life, whether personal or related to business. Shane was the best man at my wedding and godfather to my daughter Nicole. While I was living abroad as an international executive, he visited me in every country I lived in. Plus we vacationed in Turkey, Montreal, and New Orleans together. Together we watched the New York Giants win four Super Bowls and the Yankees win countless World Series. Through all the fun and heartaches, Shane was always there to help me and support me with his encouragement, advice, and celebration. His generosity had no limit. I wish for everyone to have a Shane in their life.

Early on in my career, I had my first Myers–Briggs assessment, and later I learned even more the through LSI (Life Styles Inventory). These tools were an eye-opener, allowing me to recognize my strengths and weaknesses. I am forever thankful to Colgate-Palmolive's human resources department for bringing these tools to my attention. Myers – Briggs is based on the conceptual theory that people experience the world using four principal psychological functions – sensation, intuition, feeling, and thinking – and that one of these four functions is dominant for a person most of the time. The four categories are Introversion/Extraversion, Sensing/Intuition, Thinking/Feeling, Judging/Perception. Each person is said to have one preferred quality from each category, producing 16 unique types

I have taken these assessments multiple times over thirty-five years, and my score has consistently shown that I am an ESTJ. The only variation is that one of the functions in my private life changes as I dislike planning detailed vacations and prefer a lot more freedom to discover. The self-realization afforded me by these assessments was a priceless education, but more important was that I realized why I had little patience for others.

As a young, energetic executive, I wanted to achieve results and grew frustrated with others who were not on the same page. Over time, I learned that people picture the same situation very differently depending on how they are wired, and I learned that basically you can categorize people's behaviors into four quadrants. I realize this is an overgeneralization and that people are a lot more complex, but it is an approach that has always helped me better understand others. After spending a few hours with someone, I come to learn that they are either (1) prone to action, (2) cautiously analytical, (3) big picture thinkers, or (4) oriented toward human feelings.

Early on in my career, I heavily favored taking action and was drawn to others who thought the same way. I had little patience for those folks whom I labeled as procrastinators. It turns out they were just analytical thinkers who wanted more data points before making an informed decision, sacrificing speed for additional analysis. And those people whom I perceived to be unfocused scatterbrains turned out to be great visionaries, although they had little interest in implementing projects because they would move on to the next big idea. And then there were the tree huggers with little focus on the bottom line, but they provided something positive, for example, the implications on everyone's welfare. As I have matured, I have learned to balance myself. I work on improving my analytical, strategic, and welfare skills. Although I remain an action-oriented individual, I have high awareness of the other three essential skills and of their importance to success.

So how do you surround yourself with the right people? The first step is to recognize your strengths and then surround yourself with people who complement your weaknesses. Ego is the anesthesia that deadens the pain of stupidity; we must first admit that we are not good at all things. We were all created equal, but we are very differently gifted, although our tendency is to surround ourselves with like-minded individuals. I think corporations even have a word for it: *chemistry.*

Colgate-Palmolive had just appointed me to my first international assignment, and I was part of the Eastern European oral care team. During a meeting in Poland, we were discussing the rollout—the implementation plan—across the region. Jack, from our corporate marketing department, and I both attended this meeting. He and I had chemistry, like-minded with action-oriented thinking. I recall there were about fifteen executives in the meeting from different Eastern European countries, but Jack and I pretty much hijacked the meeting to further our action-packed agenda. We were very efficient handing out assignments and setting time lines, but about three hours into the meeting, I suddenly became aware of the uneasiness in the room and noticed numerous dismayed looks from other executives. Jack and I had been so busy advancing our action-packed agenda that we had dismissed the concerns of many other individuals in the room who were not like-minded, and in the process we lost the support of several team members. Some questioned the strategy, while others wanted more analysis. Some thought we were moving too quickly and in haste. It was a great lesson. For a talented team to work together, everyone's input must be valued, even if people perceive the problem and solution differently. The end goal must be the same, but healthy debate with different perspectives will lead to better solutions.

Contrast that with more than twenty years later, when I was CEO of Strauss's international coffee division. Acquisitions were a key part of our growth strategy, and we were in the final phases of negotiations with a local Brazilian company we were about to acquire. There was a lot of emotion driving this deal, and this emotion had to be balanced with a sensible approach. Adi was from the corporate team, leading the business group this acquisition would fall under. He clearly supported the deal. He was a high-energy person prone to action, and at times it was comical watching him during longer meetings. Adi would get up and pace the room as he could not sit for more than thirty minutes. He could not wait to get started with the acquisition. Eyal, also from the corporate team, had a strong analytical mindset. He had prepared a meticulous analysis, laying out the pros or cons, and had a very different view of the acquisition than Adi. Matty, also from the corporate team, was the sensing type, and he too looked at the acquisition through a different prism. Erez, who was the CEO of the Strauss Group and a great strategist, looked at the deal from a strategic perspective.

There were about ten people on the team, and we had a balanced representation of the four key groups: (1) prone to action, (2) cautiously analytical, (3) big picture strategic thinkers, and (4) oriented toward human feelings. Our objective was the same, to acquire companies aligned with our vision and to support our strategic growth. There is no right or wrong answer as to which type of thinking is better; it is just important to recognize the difference. Depending on the circumstance, one type of reasoning may trump another.

Erez would always canvass everyone before the final decision. We would go around the room, each of us voting yes or no and stating either our support or our objection. Erez reserved the right to cast the final vote himself, so he would go last, acknowledging everyone's reservations and putting everyone at ease. He understood the circle of trust would not be violated if everyone's concerns were addressed no matter the end decision. As leader of the international division, I went second to last. After I'd listened to all the reasons from the different people, it was my turn. I made my decision based on a sensing element this time.

Although this company was a good strategic fit and analysis supported the acquisition, I voted no for one compelling reason. Everyone before me who had voted yes represented our corporate group, and the only two people who had voted no were the local general manager and finance manager. If we were to acquire this company, it would be absorbed into the local team. This was not going to be a remote project. I just did not see how this acquisition would work if the local leadership did not support it, having other priorities. Erez saw things the same way and also voted against the project. It was disappointing after the effort we had invested, including the due diligence, but it was the right decision. The beauty of the process was that there were no heated arguments, and everyone accepted the decision. The key is to get people to appreciate each other's talents; otherwise, things have the potential to become one big mess. Everyone respected each other's opinions and what each person in the room had been gifted with. When a team has that balance, the right decisions are easy to make by following the process.

> Infinite diversity in infinite combinations ... symbolizing the elements that create truth and beauty.
> —*Commander Spock, Star Trek*

Diversity is essential to a team's success. In the previous section, I described how people are wired different and how their approach to problem solving will fall into one of four general quadrants. Another dynamic that steers decision-making is a person's upbringing and culture. I am privileged to be a member of Wharton Fellows program, an Executive Education program to provide ongoing learning opportunities that explore highly relevant, timely issues with a focus on transformational leadership. In 2002 I joined a group of other Wharton Fellows to visit several successful companies headquartered in Seattle. We visited Microsoft, Costco, and Starbucks. Starbucks welcomed us, and in addition to just sharing their history and future plans, their executive team took the opportunity to pick our brains and put us to work. At this juncture, Starbucks was well established in the USA and was looking at rapid international expansion.

They broke us up into groups of ten and asked us the same questions about their expansion plans. Each group was to present its findings. I represented our group. We did have several recommendations, but the one I hammered home was a simple thought. I looked at Starbucks's executive team and saw that not one person was international. Every one of their C-suite executives was from the USA—highly qualified, but all American. My suggestion was simple: if Starbucks wanted to be successful in expanding internationally, they had better build a diverse international executive team. I could see Orin Smith and his team huddling up as I made my point, asking, "Who is this guy?" The message was well received, but I'm not sure Starbucks ever put it into practice.

As an expatriate, I was fortunate to meet executives from all over the world. It gave me a different perception of diversity that people were not accustomed to in the USA. I met business leaders from Zimbabwe, South Africa, and Nigeria, from New Zealand and Australia, from Japan, China, India, and Korea, from Brazil and Mexico, and from multiple European countries. Their physical characteristics matched the region they originated from. In all the time I spent with them, never did we have a conversation similar to the discussions about diversity I hear in USA and the media. Phrases like *white privilege* or *black lives matter* are fed by a media frenzy of falsehoods to divide people for their own personal agenda. In a boardroom, I've never heard that phrase, regardless of what color people were in the room. I believe those discussions are more about economic imbalance, not race or gender diversity. Diversity disparities seem to disappear in affluent circles.

Stephen Covey said, "We see the world not as it is, but as we are." There is natural tendency for every human being of every race and each gender to see the world through his or her own lens. It is prevalent and it is global as we identify with people most like us. In his book the Third Option, Miles McPherson describes how as a black teenager growing up in Jamaica Queens New York, he was chased by a group of white kids yelling racial slurs at him. I also grew up as a teenager in Jamaica Queens New York and had different experience when a group of black kids ganged up on me yelling racial slurs at me. Miles and I formed different perceptions of the same neighborhood based on our different experience. Somehow, we both ended up in San Diego. Miles founded the Rock Church and is the head pastor. I'm an active member of the Rock leading the Business Roundtable Ministry. We both recognize there is racial divide and I think the way Miles defines the way forward in The Third Option is brilliant.

I was in Thailand helping build new factory automation for Colgate-Palmolive's manufacturing center. Bob was the VP of operations, an expatriate white guy from New Jersey. He was in a serious relationship with a young woman from an affluent local family in Bangkok. His potential future father-in-law did not endorse the relationship as Bob did not meet the family's standards. Being that

Bob was an American white guy, many people saw his potential
father in laws rejection of the relationship as racist. There may have
been an element of truth to that, but the real obstacle was that Bob
was just an executive from a modest family. It was the economic
standard that Bob did not meet. If Bob's last name were Rockefeller,
I'm sure he would have passed that test with flying colors regardless
of his nationality or the color of his skin.

True diversity is international diversity as different cultures
approach business and life challenges very differently. Diversity is
not just about black or white. It is inclusive of all races, nationalities,
religions, and genders as everyone sees the world a little different.
But once a diverse team is assembled, shares the same culture, and
believes in the same vision it becomes a powerful force. Load up
a conference room with executives from the Middle East, Brazil,
and Poland and witness the power of diverse thinking. To have a
successful C-suite, I suggest assembling your inner circle to include
people with different skill sets and also different international
backgrounds. Fortune 500 companies have come a long way in the
last twenty-five years with CEOs originating from all parts of the
globe and having their inner circles well-balanced.

One of the most common mistakes I see leaders make is to surround
themselves with like-minded individuals. I was conducting a
leadership workshop for a small boutique bank that was struggling
to identify a growth strategy. Now I get that the banking industry
tends to be risk averse and errs on the side of caution, but all
businesses have to take some risk if they want to grow. However,
the lack of diverse thinking on this team was alarming. The team

leader was very cautiously analytical and had surrounded himself with all like-minded people. I could not identify one person on this team who was prone to action or big picture strategic thinking. This team was stuck in analysis paralysis, scrutinizing any new idea so severely that everything was doomed to potential failure. The challenge was not to identify strategic growth initiatives but how to get the team leader to realize the limitations of the team he had put together. Unless this bank were to rebuild the team and embrace diverse thinking, finding a growth strategy was unlikely.

> The greatest leader is not necessarily the one who does the greatest things. He is the one that gets the people to do the greatest things.
> —*Ronald Reagan*

Managers do things right, whereas leaders do the right things. Companies spend their sizable budgets on training people in developing skills in sales, marketing, finance, and so forth, but when it comes to developing leaders, they invest very little and unfortunately many times set people up for failure. The higher up you go in the managerial food chain, the more you find that, at best, 20 percent of your success is the result of your core technical skills and 80 percent of your success is the result of your leadership skills.

I was speaking with Mack Story, a coaching colleague, who said something I loved: "Companies hire you for what you know and fire you for who you are." You do not move into the C suite only because you are a marketing or finance expert; you get to the C suite because you are a great leader of people.

Once you form a balanced team of people who complement each other with the four different skill sets, it is time to invest in making your team members better leaders.

In 1994, as the operations director for Colgate-Palmolive, I was spearheading the acquisition of Fabulon, a well-recognized local brand and body care company. The company had evolved during the communist era with a lot of the managerial habits unique to that culture. It was one of my first meetings with the Fabulon managerial team after the acquisition, and the culture just astonished me. As we were beginning to discuss our plans to integrate the products and the teams postacquisition, it was awkward because only one side was participating. The Colgate team, comprised of young recent college graduates, was fully engaged in the discussion, while the Fabulon team, who had grown up during the communist era, was very passive. After a while I turned to one of the Fabulon managers and asked how she envisioned the integration. I was floored by her answer: "You have to tell us. You are the boss." She was a highly educated woman with a doctorate in her field, yet she had no initiative or accountability to make this company a success. It is so sad to see a generation of wasted talent because of a communist mentality with people simply not providing an incentive system to prod employees to succeed.

In 1991, when I arrived in Hungary, I was struck by the number of people with postgraduate degrees in the workforce. I later realized that under communism, for the society as a whole, there was a lack of incentive to advance in the workforce, so people had chosen to increase their status through academia. The workforce rated very high when it came to technical skill sets, but there was a huge leadership vacuum. Seeing an opportunity to develop our next generation of leaders, I put in place a mentorship program for the younger local managers with strong incentives to succeed. *Accountability, initiative, ownership,* and *respect* became common words to use, but it took a generation to get rid of the adverse practices inbred by the corrupt communist regime.

Crisis doesn't make us; it reveals who we are. Former mayor of New York Rudy Giuliani showed us how great leaders act during a crisis. The 9/11 tragedy happened on his watch. In its wake, New York became a better place and New Yorkers became better people. Rudy's father used to say to him, "Whenever you get into a jam, whenever you get into a crisis or an emergency, become the calmest person in the room and you'll be able to figure your way out of it." Crisis requires adaptability, and there is always an answer if you are persistent and keep an open mind. Rudy had a great team, and he had mandatory meetings with all his direct reports each Monday morning to discuss a detailed agenda of important issues. He would always be the first to arrive and the last to leave, and he believed that he should never ask someone to do something he was not willing to do himself. He modeled a hands-on leadership style I use to this day, knowing the facts but trusting my team to deliver. In the wise words of Ronald Reagan, "Trust but verify."

I would meet regularly each Monday with my inner circle as a team to discuss issues and solutions. It was an opportunity to raise awareness on new competitive, financial, sales, marketing, or operational issues impacting our company. Additionally, I would invest my time in meeting one-on-one with each individual in my inner circle to make sure we had the chance to discuss any obstacles or opportunities relevant to each of them. This also helped me to understand how I could support my inner circle and help them achieve their plans. Best of all, it provided a platform for us to get to know each other on a deeper level and to form long-term friendships.

Having an inner circle is a great start, but it is not enough; you need to cultivate and grow those relationships. It takes effort and time; relationships are not formed in days or weeks. Eugene Habecker, in his book *The Other Side of Leadership*, writes, "The true leader serves. Serves people and their best interests. They are motivated by loving concern rather than personal glory." You can only achieve true leadership if you form close relationships with the people in your inner circle.

> You've got to give loyalty down, if you want loyalty up.
> —*Donald T. Regan*

Loyalty grows through honesty and mutual respect. I always invested my time in my inner circle, meeting with them each Monday morning for a half day together as a team and another half day each month one-on-one with each of them. During our monthly one-on-one meeting with my marketing director Paul, he asked me for my opinion on an issue. One of our bright marketing managers had been approached by a recruiter and, as a result, asked Paul for a promotion and a salary increase to stay at our company and not move on to the other one. This was starting to become a trend as Benckiser was known as a great marketing company, and we had a strong program recruiting top students from the local university and mentoring them as brand managers. Recruiters frequently approached our employees, but for the most part our employees loved working for us and were loyal.

This was the first instance where one of our best was being poached and the news had reached my office. Knowing there was no room in the budget for salary increases at that time, Paul was asking for my opinion on how we should react and what we should tell Tomas to persuade him to stay. I thought about it for what seemed like a very long time, but in reality it was probably only ten seconds. I answered, "Tell him the truth. It's always the best answer." I knew that answer in itself would not be enough, so Paul and I agreed to sit down with our star managers to explain the process. We did have succession planning in place, and the one big ticket we could offer was international assignments. We were honest with Tomas, letting him know that we had a budget for a reason and that we already had implemented salary increases earlier that year. We also laid out a path to an international career should he be interested. We offered him no guarantees, but we said we would give him strong recommendations.

I also took the opportunity to explain the process to all our managers should they become interested in international positions. Additionally, I invited each of the managers to do a series of mock interviews to help prepare them. Tomas ended up staying with our company, and in about a year he was promoted to the global marketing team. He was later promoted to marketing director in the US company and is now general manager for a coffee company back in Prague. This program helped launch the international careers of several young managers, who are all highly successful senior executives today. Jiri now leads a multinational billion-dollar company and continues to rise in the global C-suite arena. Romana is the North American divisional controller for Reckitt Benckiser.

My honesty with Paul established two things: first, a pathway to retain good talent, and second, equally important, a stronger bond between me and Paul. Can you imagine if I had made up some phony story for Paul and gave him bad advice about what he should say to Tomas? How credible would be my words be the next time Paul had questions? Paul understood that by my being honest with him, he could count on me for support. Honesty is always the best course of action.

> If you pick the right people and give them the opportunity to spread their wings and put compensation as a carrier behind it you almost don't have to manage them.
> —*Jack Welch*

Once you have a strong inner circle and you have formed good relationships, it is only natural that you care enough to make sure your team members are well rewarded. I would like to make the distinction between reward and compensation. Some companies focus on salary and bonuses, while others are skewed toward recognition. Successful companies strike a balance and do both. One of my employers, Benckiser, before it merged with Reckitt and Coleman, had a very aggressive salary and bonus structure. Their compensation structure was a key recruitment piece, while marketing freedom was another. There were some instances of recognition, like their annual general managers' conference, where one year even spouses were invited to Singapore. But for the most part, it was all about high performance and aggressive monetary rewards.

My other employer Strauss struck a good balance between recognition and compensation. The combination of salary, bonus, and stock options made for an attractive compensation package. The first year after I'd joined the Strauss Group, Kathy and I decided to spend our winter vacation and New Year's Eve in Eilat, Israel. When Michael Strauss found out we were vacationing in Israel, he made a gracious gesture that spoke volumes vis-à-vis recognition. During our Eilat vacation, not only did Michael Strauss grant us use of his yacht, along with the crew, but also Ofra Strauss helped us put together a vacation with tours of the desert and camel rides. Together with Erez, she even flew to Eilat to join us for a family dinner. Each morning the captain would meet us to board the yacht and discover the Red Sea, either to parasail, ride a Jet Ski, or scuba dive with dolphins. But the highlight for my daughters was a tour to the Strauss chocolate factory in Nazareth, where they had a blast eating chocolate and chewing bubble gum right off the production lines. After a full day of stuffing themselves with sweets, they found, once we'd returned to the King David Hotel, two gift baskets full of chocolate and candy awaiting them. We were laughing so hard that the girls were rolling on the floor. The Strauss family's gesture to welcome us to Israel and to grace us with their gifts spoke volumes of their caring and recognition and helped build a foundation of loyalty. Recognition does not cost much, but balanced with an aggressive compensation package, it goes a long way.

When you are in someone's inner circle, be thankful he or she chose you, go along for the ride, and contribute and learn as much as you can. I have lived in six countries and have worked on every continent except Antarctica, so I have been blessed to see a lot of the world. Istanbul has always been one of my favorite cities. Since 1992 I've made dozens of trips to Turkey, first as a Colgate representative and later as a Benckiser executive. Swissôtel overlooking the Bosphorus was one of my favorite hotels until I experienced staying at the Ciragan Palace Kempinski. The Dolmabaçhe Palace is equal in grandeur to Versailles or Schönbrunn, and the Topkapı Palace is as vast as any European castle or the Kremlin. The Blue Mosque, the Basilica Cistern, and the Hagia Sophia are just as breathtaking as the basilicas of Saint Peter or Saint Paul and the cathedrals of Milan or Seville. Traces of the Ottoman Empire are still evident in modern Turkey, not only in physical riches but also in culture.

Over the course of numerous visits with different companies, I noticed the Turkish feudal mentality that mandates a strong figurehead lead the nation, a company, or a family. Over the years, I became good friends with Caner, who was the general manager of Benckiser Turkey. He was an extremely accomplished person and equally generous with his friendship and mentoring. Caner loved being the father figure, the top guy, and the head of his company, his family, and his friends. To gain his favor, all one had to do was to show respect and acknowledge he was in charge. Challenge his authority and you could kiss your success goodbye. This made a lot of sense to me as Caner was very knowledgeable and also well-connected in the industry. He was a close ally in many conference room clashes, and he made countless introductions to further my success.

When I became CEO at Strauss's international division, I asked Caner to help me as an adviser for both our Turkish subsidiary and our company's overall marketing strategy. I always valued Caner's opinion. He provided sound counsel and helped the Turkish company reach critical mass. I was grateful for his friendship and support. He also helped plan one of our best family vacations, an eight-day Blue Voyage cruise along the Turkish Mediterranean coast. We met Caner in the coastal town of Göcek and spent a day aboard his yacht before departing on our private cruise. We boarded an eighty-foot wooden sailing vessel with a crew of four and headed north, eventually landing in Bodrum. Over the eight days, we discovered ancient cities from 2000 BC, the clear waters of the Mediterranean, and ports like Marmaris, and we feasted daily on fresh-caught seafood. To this day, I have never seen such clear skies with millions of bright stars visible to the naked eye. Although our sailboat did have six small cabins, we chose to sleep on deck each night under the stars. It is a memory our family cherishes to this day. Caner and I were in each other's inner circle, supporting and helping each other. However, I acknowledged Caner was the father figure and was my mentor; otherwise our relationship would never have flourished.

We all know people, but it is always who we know. Some people may be more important to know than others regardless of their social status. You should always strive to be part of the Semper Fi team. The marines can be your best friends or your worst enemies. I preferred them to be my best friends; they recognized our faces and knew us by name. In each overseas assignment, we always made it a priority to get to know the marines who were in charge of guarding the embassy. In case there was a major political or security issue and we had to come running to the embassy for safe haven, we wanted to make sure the marines would immediately recognize us.

Kathy was also always an active member of the local International Women's Club, and we would be invited to the local marines open house for friends and family. It was here that Kathy, I, and our girls got to know and have a lot fun with the marines. The two most important black-tie parties in each country were the International Women's Charity Ball and the US Marines annual birthday party. We attended this wonderful event in each country we lived in, even getting to meet General Jim Jones when he joined the marines' ball in Holland held in the Queen's Ballroom, a first as it was not open to the public. What a spectacular venue. The marine balls always started off very formal with a reading, speeches, a flag ceremony, and cutting of the marine birthday cake, but by the end of the evening the marines would be dancing on the tables, lighting it up. After the ball, we joined General Jones downtown till the wee hours of the morning, doing shots at the bar and talking up a storm. Marines know how to party and have fun.

But the most memorable marine ball venue was in Prague, hosted at the Ambassador's Residence. Kathy's father, Jack, had come to visit us, and since he was the oldest US Marine in attendance, he was honored to cut the cake. From my limited perspective, as I have only been to five Ambassador's Residences, I think that by far the residence in Prague is the most glorious with a rich history. It is a breathtakingly massive 143-room villa, three floors with an elevator and a huge ballroom that can host hundreds. The ballroom has floor-to-ceiling windows and these windows can retract into the floor and open the space onto a huge terrace. There is a private cinema room and a humongous swimming pool in the basement with its own historical importance. The house was originally built by one of three brothers, Otto, who was in competition with his other brothers to see who could build the biggest luxury villa. The Petscheks, who were a Jewish family, had to abandon everything and flee as the Nazis invaded Prague. Funny how power was distributed after World War II; the Russians got one of the brothers' villas, while the Americans received Otto's villa for their ambassador. I could devote a chapter to nothing but my stories about marines, ambassadors, and International Women's Club events. Build your inner circle to make sure you're safe and secure and able to have a lot of fun.

> If you help people get what they want then
> you'll receive everything you need in life.
> —*Zig Ziglar*

Servant leadership builds cohesive teams, and a leader needs to understand it's not about him or her but about something much bigger. Oftentimes we confuse leadership with dictatorship. A dictator gives out orders and does not take into account the wants and needs of others. A servant leader is the complete opposite, working tirelessly to develop his or her people while being focused on what he or she can do for others. To be a great leader, you need to let go and invest in your team so you can empower them to succeed.

At one time Colgate-Palmolive had a slogan: "People are our most important asset." Funny how people are never reflected on the balance sheet as an asset. Instead they appear on the P&L as a payroll expense and on the balance sheet as a payable account, which is a liability. As a CEO, I always thought I had the easiest job in the room. First, my job was to make sure our company culture was paramount and our vision was clear and to walk the talk in reinforcing both these things. Second, it was my job to ensure that our growth strategy supported our vision and culture. Third, I was the one to ensure that each person on our team had the resources needed to be successful. These resources may have been support, assets, funding, training, accountability, or—most important— mentoring. And fourth, it was my job to communicate and connect with our employees, consumers, customers, suppliers, and partners to ensure they understood what we were doing and how it would benefit them. Successful servant leaders like Indra Nooyi, former

CEO of PepsiCo, do not just talk about shareholder value. Nooyi delivered shareholder value by serving PepsiCo customers and their communities. She recognized the growing obesity crisis and committed to reducing the sugar and sodium in PepsiCo's core snacks and sodas. It takes courage to step out and put at risk the very foundation of your company's core product, such as sugar, that drives consumption. Indra Nooyi recognized the opportunity to serve her consumer community as the obesity crisis in the United States started to affect consumer behavior. With PepsiCo leading the charge, it forced many food and beverage companies to adapt and gave rise to many new healthy food companies. Indra Nooyi helped change an industry, and in doing so she best served her shareholders.

If I were to speak with your team about their thoughts of you as a leader, what would they say?

▸ *Are you a servant leader?*

▸ *Who is in your inner circle?*

▸ *Is your team diverse with each member complementing the others' skill sets?*

▸ *Are you investing in your team?*

▸ *Are you serving as a mentor or being mentored?*

7

THE BONUS FIFTH KEY— CONNECTING WITH PEOPLE

> I think there are a lot of successful people in this country who connect amazingly well with the American people and have—and one of the reasons they are successful is because they connect well.
>
> —*Rick Santorum*

Good leaders are great communicators, but great leaders understand how to connect with people. There is a world of difference between informing, communicating, and connecting. Most people just inform others, whereas some become good communicators, but only the best understand how to connect with others. John Maxwell, Les Brown, and Nick Vujicic all have the ability to strike a chord in our hearts, connecting with us through teaching us and empowering us. Ronald Reagan and Bill Clinton were charismatic masters at connecting by way of their optimism, while Martin Luther King connected by offering us hope. Steve Jobs connected with his audience through wowing us and energizing us with his enthusiasm. The good news is that we can all learn how to better connect with others if we invest in ourselves.

Most people are good at informing others about what is important to them, but they seem not to care if the information is relevant or important to their audience. Their focus is on conveying information or data to convince others of their point of view. Unfortunately, most business presentations are delivered by people who fall into this group, so they fail to engage their audience. It is simply an information dump. I have witnessed many people in conference rooms simply tuning out or even nodding off. Even if you have not yet matured into a good communicator, you can still deliver a solid presentation that informs others.

Early on in my career, I attended a conference and witnessed a great presentation whose format I later used to help me. As I sat in the audience, the presenter opened by answering three questions: "What is the topic of my presentation? Why should you be interested? And how can you help?" As he continued through the presentation, he used the three questions to maintain his clarity and the flow of information. His presentation was powerful and clear, and it held my attention. Later that year, using that same format, I delivered a knockout presentation to Craig Tate, who was an executive VP at Colgate-Palmolive. That presentation helped launch my international career.

Although I became a good communicator, I still had a long way to go before mastering the art of connection. I was in my early thirties and was the general manager of Hungary's Philips electronics consumer products division. We were holding our annual dealer convention, having invited our employees and our customers, including spouses—about a thousand people. The venue, the Budapest Museum of Fine Arts, was breathtaking, and the museum management had allowed us to mix in and display Philips products among the paintings and statues. We built a large stage in the middle of the main hall and even hired a company to set up a small casino for after the presentations and dinner. It was a fun event that included some great food and entertainment.

I had prepared my presentation using the proven formula of mentioning what I was speaking about, why it was important for everyone there, and how they could help. Although I was successful in communicating my message, I failed to connect with the audience. My presentation was missing a key element with very few, if any, personal stories to support my message. My presentation focused on products, market share, marketing plans, and the standard business nomenclature. I did not understand the power of personal stories and how they help to connect with people's emotions. Although it was a good informative presentation that even motivated many customers, I had failed to connect with the audience. People have to be emotionally engaged to be moved and buy into you, and without personal stories that's just not possible.

> The single biggest problem in communica-
> tion is the illusion that it has taken place.
> —*George Bernard Shaw*

Before we can understand how to connect with people, we must first learn to communicate. Lack of clear expectations always leads to poor communication.

We had just moved to Hungary for my first international assignment with Colgate-Palmolive, and Kathy and I were getting ready for our first international Thanksgiving holiday. We had planned only for immediate family and figured that a fifteen-pound bird would be just fine. Now this was November 1992, before the age of supermarkets in Hungary. Back then, you went to the bakery for bread and to the butcher for meat.

There was a great little butcher not too far from our house, so we ordered a turkey from there. I spoke fluent Hungarian, but unfortunately Kathy did not, nor did the butcher speak English. Kathy asked me to write a note in Hungarian to order the turkey. The note said something like, "Dear Mr. Butcher, I would like to order a seven-kilogram turkey cleaned and ready for pickup on November 26." On Thanksgiving morning, Kathy went to the butcher to pick up the turkey. Back then she was driving our two-seat convertible Mercedes. When she arrived, the butcher presented her with a gigantic bird weighing about fifteen kilograms (about thirty-five pounds) with the neck still attached.

Being that Thanksgiving is not a holiday in Hungary, that was the only turkey in the butcher shop, so it was not open to negotiation. It was either this gigantic bird or no turkey for Thanksgiving. Kathy held out both arms while the butcher placed the bird in her hands and draped the neck of the bird over her shoulder. She carried the large animal down the block to her car with its neck swinging back and forth. She placed the bird on the front seat and properly secured in with the seat belt for the ride home. It was comical the looks of disbelief she received on the way home. But it all worked out as we scrambled last minute to invite a bunch of local friends over to join us for dinner. From that year onward, we hosted Thanksgiving dinner as an annual international tradition, inviting Americans living abroad who did not have families and mixing in with families of different nationalities who had never experienced Thanksgiving before.

To clear up the misunderstanding and find out how things had gone so wrong, I went to speak with the butcher a few days later. Simply put, the expectations were not clear on either side. First, the American definition of a cleaned turkey is very different from the local Hungarian definition of *cleaned*. In Hungary, a cleaned turkey basically means the feathers have been plucked, the neck is still attached, and the inner organs have been removed. Second, although I had requested a seven-kilogram bird, it was interpreted as a directional number. The butcher was not aware of our oven size limitations and thought he was doing us a favor by getting a much larger bird than we'd requested. Communication between me and the butcher was unclear as we were both working with a different set of assumptions. So remember to set clear expectations to ensure everyone is on the same page.

Once, Kathy and I spent two glorious weeks touring the Irish countryside. We drove almost two thousand kilometers in a country that is only about three hundred kilometers wide, making a big circle around the island, starting in Dublin, heading south on the east coast, then driving north along the west coast before heading back to Dublin. We had the experience of a lifetime. I have never seen so much green, so many castles, or so many sheep in one country. The Irish had perfected the farm-to-table concept, and Guinness never tasted so good anywhere else in the world. We learned about history, the Celtic Irish, Vikings, Normans, and British, about Catholics vs. Protestants, about the potato famine, and about Irish independence, and we listened to music in Irish, English, and hundreds of dialects.

The Giant's Causeway, the Cliffs of Moher, and the Galway oysters were all spectacular, but what I loved most were the people. Everyone in Ireland speaks with you. The person sitting at the next table and people just walking in the street stop to say hello and talk. We met David while waiting for the ferry in Greencastle. Walking with his dog, he had stopped to talk with us for twenty minutes about how he'd met his wife just a few streets over. He asked about our trip and made some great recommendations. But Shamus, a friend we met in Dingle pub, summed it up best (and you have to imagine hearing this in an Irish accent) when he said, "If you are British, you board the same train to go to work for twenty years, sitting next to the same person and never speaking to them." The

Irish will look a stranger in the eye, say good morning, and share their stories. Sharing our stories is how we communicate, how we get to know each other, and it makes us all better human beings as a result. You do not need to kiss the Blarney Stone to be a better communicator; just be willing to share your stories with others and to listen to theirs.

To better connect with people, start by putting yourself in their shoes. Instead of asking people to come to you, you should meet them where they are. Adopt their perspective first before you expect them to adopt yours. Simon Sinek said it best: "Listening is not understanding the words of the question asked; listening is understanding why the question was asked in the first place." My first job when I graduated as an engineer was with Colgate-Palmolive as a shift supervisor in the Jersey City oral care production plant. I was responsible for manufacturing toothpaste, and the factory was operating three shifts per day. Each month I was responsible for one week's worth of running the shift from 12:00 midnight to 8:00 a.m. One day when I was on the midnight shift, my department manager informed me there was a factory tour scheduled for the next day and that Reuben Mark, Colgate's CEO, would be visiting.

Our priority for that night changed from production to making sure everything was neat with no clutter, shiny and clean, with the machines properly tuned for the next morning. We spent eight hours prepping the place to make it look perfect for the next morning. I stuck around after my shift to witness the commotion. About 9:30 a.m., a group of about twenty executives in suits, all clinging together, walked through. They stopped by one machine for thirty seconds and then moved on. I did not recognize any of the suits and was not sure if they had ever visited the factory. It was comical that we had spent eight hours preparing when no one seemed to care about the production facility. It reminded me of when I coached my daughter's junior girls' soccer team. I called something I'd seen "the beehive effect." Wherever the ball would go, you would find all the girls bunched up and chasing each other and the ball. It was a challenge to get any of them to go to the open field and have them pass the ball to each other. I thought, *What a waste of time prepping for a bunch of executives in suits trying to suck up to the CEO.*

Later in my career, when I was appointed CEO of the Strauss Group's international division, I spent a lot of time visiting the local companies, which included touring their manufacturing facilities. I recalled that Colgate experience and took a very different approach. As I toured the factory with the local managers, I always took time to meet with people on the production floor, thanking them for their hard work and asking them how we could make things better. Sometimes they were speechless, not having expected a question like that, but many times I did get some suggestions. I would always make a note, and during the business review with the local managers, I would table the suggestions. We would discuss each suggestion, and no matter if it was a good idea or a bad idea, it was the local manager's responsibility to get back to the employee with feedback on his or her suggestion. If the suggestion was adopted, we thanked the employee, and if not, we told them why not. I met those people literally where they were on the production floor and listened to them. I also made sure they knew their ideas were valued because there was follow-up. It was a great way to connect with everyone at the local subsidiary. I did the same exercise, visiting customers with the local sales team, also connecting with them. As a result, we derived a lot of success from asking for and receiving their help whenever we were launching a new product or project.

> Leadership is not as much about knowing the right answers, as it is about knowing the right questions!
> —*Bob Tiede*

It was my ninth year working at Colgate-Palmolive, counting the part-time jobs I'd had while still in college, and I'd had many challenging job performance reviews with at least five different bosses. Colgate-Palmolive had a mandatory five-page evaluation form developed by the human resources department. After nine years, I was very familiar with the process and the evaluation form. It was like going to the dentist: it hurt like heck while you were there, but you felt much better after the visit.

It was my first year working for Dr. Frank Morelli, and we were heading to a conference in Chicago. Frank had asked me to prepare for my annual performance review, saying that we would discuss it while we were on this trip. I was prepared, having used the standard five-page form. Anticipating many of the standard questions, I had rehearsed my answers, including why I was doing a great job. Frank suggested we meet in the lounge before dinner and go over my evaluation.

Initially I was caught off guard as all my previous reviews had taken place in a formal setting with two people sitting on either side of a desk. This was my first performance review relaxing in a lounge and sipping cocktails.

Just as I was anticipating a debate, Frank turned the tables on me and simply asked, "How do you think you did this year?" Talk about a game changer. You've heard the old adage "Never ask a question you already don't know the answer to"? Of course Frank knew the answer, but rather than kicking off a debate, he gave me the opportunity to shape the discussion. Frank also knew me well enough to understand that I was very driven and hard on myself. I was my harshest critic. All he had to do was listen. After I'd given my answer, he took the opportunity to build me up and tell me how good I was. Total role reversal. His plan was brilliant. I became the bad guy, and Frank was the good guy in my own performance review.

The only small debate we had was about identifying a development plan and agreeing on my personal targets. I enjoyed the process so much that it is a formula I have used ever since. Great leaders ask great questions. By doing so, leaders make you think. Your feel that your ideas are valued, you become part of the process, and they get your total buy-in. It is one of the best ways to build connections with people.

It is much easier to connect with people when you listen to their needs, show them that you care, and help them with their challenges. We met the greatest people while living overseas—some are still very close friends. In 2001 we were living in England, and our daughters were attending TASIS American School in England. Although moving was never easy, this was our fourth international posting. Over time we had figured out how to streamline the process of settling into a new country. Kathy and other TASIS parents who also had multiple relocations under their belt suggested setting up a host network to welcome and support new families who had just moved to the area.

Talk about meeting people where they are. Imagine having just moved to a new country and trying to establish yourself so that you can live a rewarding life for the next few years. What a blessing to have someone give you a welcoming hug, take you by the hand, and help you get settled in. This was how we met the Alderton family, who had just moved to England from New Jersey for their first international assignment. We were their host family, and boy were they in for a surprise when they met us. We remain close friends; our friendship has endured the test of time across many miles.

Kathy and Lee hit it off immediately, but Jeff, who was a senior partner at Deloitte, was hard at work, so it took awhile before the two families could all get together. Our daughters Nicole and Taylor were in the same grade, and they are also still close friends. The first time I met Lee, it was a little awkward. My car was in for repairs, so Kathy and I had to share a vehicle. Kathy had made arrangements to take Lee to Costco in London. I turned out to be the designated driver. While Kathy and Lee were chatting in the back seat, I received an important call from our Italian business partner. It was difficult to drive, carry on a phone discussion, and tune out the two women who were chirping and laughing in the back. I finally turned around and said, "Would you two please shush up while I finish this phone call?"

Kathy has always been outspoken. Lee sometimes jokes that at first she was afraid of her. Now Lee was meeting me for the first time, and I had come off even more aggressive than Kathy, so Lee was not feeling very blessed to have us as her host family. When the four of us were finally able to meet for dinner, although Jeff had already met Kathy and liked her, Lee had forewarned Jeff that I was not the most pleasant individual and he may not like me. We had a wonderful dinner. After sharing a few bottles of wine, we kicked off a lifelong friendship. Jeff and Lee visited us many times in the different places we have lived, and we have all had fun times together touring wine country and celebrating their kids' weddings. We all connected because my wife and I met Jeff and Lee where they were and saw where their need was. We did not give them a book or links to a website for best practices; instead we took the time to make them feel welcome and helped them settle in.

There are three fundamental questions everyone asks themselves before they engage in any business transaction. The first of these is "Do you care for me?" meaning "Are you listening to my problems and challenges, or are you just trying to sell me what you have?" The second is "Can you help me?" meaning "Does the product or service you are offering solve the problem I've been telling you about?" The third is "Can I trust you?" meaning "Will the solution you are offering work—and at a fair price?"

One of my first jobs while I was still in high school was working in a retail store for the Christmas season. I loved helping people pick out products for the holidays. Unknowingly I was answering those same three questions.

When I was a general manager in Prague, I was meeting with our largest customers, and it was still the same three questions. First I listened to their concerns about slow-moving products, products sitting on store shelves taking up too much space, inadequate profit margins, and their customers not being pleased with some items. I then promised that our products would help them achieve the sales and profit margins they needed to meet their business plans. I also asked them to invest in adequate inventory to meet the expected consumer demand. Last, I assured them they could trust us to support our products with substantial media and promotional backing to ensure exponential sales. As we delivered on our promises time after time, our shelf space, promotional activity, and market shares rose to new heights, which allowed us to launch one new brand each year, along with several brand extensions.

When I became CEO, our primary growth strategy involved mergers and acquisitions, and the same three questions were relevant here. As I sat across the table, I listened to small business owners glowingly speak about their achievements and their concern about losing control of something they had worked so hard to build. I realized that although they wanted a payday, mentally they were not yet ready to let go. Knowing this, we formulated our offers so as to give them a moderate payday, a stake in running the business, and an upside when they were finally ready to cash out.

These local owners trusted us with a solution that addressed their main concern. It was a magical formula that served us well in our acquisition quest. Strauss always walked away with the deal while Sara Lee and others continued to come up short.

> Eat to please thyself, but dress to please others.
>
> —*Benjamin Franklin*

There are many ways to connect with others, including through body language, manner of speaking, and appearance. Do not underestimate your dress code when it comes to making a connection. In the armed services, everyone wears a uniform. Motorcycle riders, especially those who own Harleys, all wear a similar "uniform." Doctors, nurses, and janitors also have a uniform code. It is a function of fitting in.

In 2005, I had just moved to San Francisco and had opened my own coffee distribution business. This was my first venture since leaving the corporate world after more than thirty years. My business model was mostly direct sales and service, so I spent most of my time visiting existing customers and potential new customers. Each day I would venture off to conquer my daily meetings. I was still accustomed to wearing a suit and tie from my corporate days. It was challenging early on to close deals. Sometimes I felt I could not close a barn door.

One day I was sharing my difficulties with Mark. He turned to me and said, "It is obvious why you cannot close a sale. Look at the way you are dressed; people cannot relate to you."

I did not understand his comment and was confused. I quickly answered, "What is wrong with the way I am dressed? I am wearing a nice designer suit and tie."

He simply answered, "Look around you." We happened to be standing in one of the more prestigious San Francisco law firms, yet many of the people were dressed in jeans and T-shirts. It was the same at high-tech companies and most other companies. San Francisco is an extremely casual city, and everyone dresses vary casual. Once I understood this, I also dressed casual, and deals started materializing overnight.

In 1987, I was working on a major factory automation project in Kansas City. Our Colgate colleague Larry, an African American guy, was a very sharp dresser. After work one day, a group of us went out to dinner, and Larry, as usual, was wearing a tan designer suit with matching oxford shoes. The rest of us were wearing casual clothes with some of us even in jeans. After dinner, we decided to go for drinks at a local honky-tonk and dance hall with live music. As soon as we pulled into the parking lot, we should have known we were in for a laugh. In those days, most of the pickup trucks still had shotguns hanging in the back windows. As we opened the door and walked in with Larry, the band literally stopped playing and everyone stopped to stare at us. They were all wearing boots, jeans, flannel shirts, and cowboy hats, and Larry was in his tan designer suit and oxford shoes. Talk about a mismatch. Everyone had a good laugh, although we did leave shortly afterward to put Larry at ease.

Dress for success and dress to feel confident, but do not dress to intimidate others. Although you may feel good about yourself when you dress to intimidate, it may also create unnecessary barriers between you and others. To connect with others, you need to look the part.

To connect with others, do not focus on your differences; instead, focus on what you have in common. Too many people try to communicate by talking over each other, trying to convince the other party that their idea is so much better than theirs. As a result, both parties focus on their differences instead of on what they have in common. If during a discussion each person could focus on what the two of them have in common, then they could use that as a starting point to build on. It is a lot easier connecting with someone to find a win-win for both sides by starting with what you have in common with them instead of how you differ.

Olaf, the general manager of Strauss's Ukraine subsidiary, invited me to spend a day on his boat before an upcoming business review. I flew in a day early, and we spent the Sunday fishing upstream from Kiev on the Dnieper River. Then we cruised downstream for a spectacular view of the city to end the day. It was a beautiful sunny day, and although we did not catch any fish, we did enjoy some great local beer. Danny, our local CFO, also joined us, and it came up in discussion that his dad was in the sturgeon business. My eyes lit up as I love caviar, but good-quality caviar was way too expensive in Europe. I asked Danny that if he could find it in his heart to ask his dad for a small portion of sturgeon caviar for me to take home. I thanked him in advance, saying I would be forever grateful, and we left the discussion there.

By Monday morning the rest of my team had arrived, and we were ready to kick off the business review. We spent the next six hours locked in a conference room discussing business plans. We were obviously focusing on our differences as we were nowhere near agreeing on a plan that met our corporate and local objectives. At four o'clock in the afternoon, Olaf wisely stood up and called a time-out, wanting us to take a break. He walked out of the room and returned five minutes later with a serving cart. On the cart were two large soup bowls, one filled with red caviar and the other filled with black caviar. Also on the cart was a chilled bottle of Russian Standard vodka, toast, and butter. Well, this group of adult business executives quickly turned into a bunch of twelve-year-olds who had just found themselves in a candy store with a free pass. We wasted no time, applying some butter on the small pieces of toast, adding a healthy dose of caviar, and chasing it with chilled vodka.

After laughing and exchanging stories for about an hour, we resumed the business review, and miraculously we resolved all our differences and agreed on a working plan. We had struck common ground and connected through our enjoyment of some very expensive caviar and vodka. Once we had reached common ground, no matter how insignificant it seemed in light of the business review, it was easy to build on our relationship and resolve our differences. Always start with what you have in common with the other person, instead of focusing on your differences.

It is much easier to connect with people when you keep things simple. Some people think that the more complicated they make things appear, the more intelligent they will seem. That may be true, but making oneself look intelligent has never helped anyone connect better with others. If anything, it creates a barrier. The sign of a wise person is his or her ability to make something that is complex seem simple so that everyone can understand. Wisdom trumps intelligence all day.

Dr. Ben Carson is highly intelligent and is also a very wise person. He says, "You need both knowledge and wisdom. But I know a lot of very knowledgeable people who are not very wise, because wisdom tells you how to apply that knowledge. I seek wisdom from the Source of all wisdom, which is God. It is a matter of looking at the people around you who are successful, looking at the people around you who are not successful, and figuring out the traits that tend to characterize the unsuccessful people and the traits that tend to characterize the successful people. And if you can then learn from that—inculcate that into your pattern of life—you are a wise person."

I read an article the other day about a report that had come out of Rockefeller University and the University of Basel, Switzerland, and was published in the journal *Human Evolution*. The researchers studied the DNA of five million animals, including humans, to come to their conclusions. The research shows that humans have very low genetic diversity and few variants within the species, similar to many other animals. The study revealed that all humans are descendants of the same man and woman who lived between one hundred thousand and two hundred thousand years ago. I am sure many intelligent people invested a lot of time and resources to complete that study with a clear conclusion. A wise person would have just read the Bible, which clearly concludes that all humans originated from Adam and Eve. The Bible was designed as easy-to-read material so everyone can comprehend it and gain wisdom from it. God kept it simple. So should we.

People want to connect with those who inspire them. The United States of America is a country of optimism. We Americans look up to successful people. We are inspired by those who overcome challenges; we are drawn to their stories. In 2002 Kathy and I were living in Holland, where we met Mark and Susan McKeon, as all our kids attended the American School of The Hague. Mark was an attorney assigned to the international tribunal and the Slobodan Milošević war crimes trial. The McKeons were already a remarkable family, but they were about to encounter a challenge. Susan and Mark learned of a baby girl born in Latvia whose drug-addicted mother had fallen asleep and dropped a cigarette into the baby's crib, starting a fire that burned 50 percent of the child's body.

Mark and Susan adopted Megan, the baby girl, who had her leg amputated and had thirty-eight surgeries by the time she had graduated from high school. Megan's medical bills were adding up, and she needed another surgery in the USA. The airfare and anticipated medical costs were a burden on Susan and Mark.

Although their hearts were bottomless, their budget had limitations. Kathy and I were blessed to be living in a huge converted carriage house in Wassenaar, so we hosted a fundraising dinner, inviting the international community. Kathy did a fabulous job decorating our home with rented tables and chairs. More than fifty people attended the sit-down dinner at $100 per plate. I dusted off my ten-gallon kettle and made my signature open-fire Hungarian *gulyas*, along with some other tasty surprises. Our kids served the guests. The event was a bigger hit than any five-star restaurant could have hosted.

When Megan returned from the surgery, it was a delight watching her grow. She was always full of energy, not realizing she had a handicap. The McKeons moved back to the USA when Megan was five, but through Susan we kept up with Megan's story. She continued to inspire us with her energy and accomplishments, ignoring her physical limitations. Today Megan is a motivational speaker and part of the Break the Barriers organization. She continues to inspire us and is a blessing to anyone who has been fortunate to meet her.

Sharing a meal is the most fundamental way to connect with others. In 2015 when we moved back to the USA, we learned about National Family Day, a day when families were encouraged to have dinner together. We found this crazy as our family had dinner together each day; at mealtime was where we shared our daily experiences and challenges. There is something about sitting at the table with others and breaking bread. It is how business relationships are built.

Business dinners are just another way of saying, *Let's get to know each other in a relaxed setting and build our relationship.*

In 1982, when I was working as an engineer for Colgate-Palmolive, I worked on a factory automation project with Italian machine manufacturers. I spent a month in Bologna, Italy, and to this day, I call Bologna the food capital of the world. Rodrigo is the best restaurant in Bologna. It was there that I met new business friends and gained an appreciation for Northern Italian food and a love for Alba truffles, raving about it to Kathy for years.

In 2013, Alex, our daughter, was studying abroad in Rome, Italy, for a semester, and Kathy, I, and Nicole visited her for Thanksgiving. We spent a few days south in Naples and Pompey, feasting on the best pizza in the world, and a few days in Rome before heading north. Kathy specifically booked a night in Bologna on the way to Milan just so we could all share the Rodrigo experience. As great as Rodrigo was in 1984, enjoying a meal with Alba truffles in 2013 together as a family was a thousand times better. As we were looking at the menu at Rodrigo, Nicole turned to me and said, "Dad, these truffle [*tortufo*] dishes cost more than the leather boots we just purchased her in Florence."

I answered, "Enjoy it. Those boots will soon wear out, but the memory of this meal will last you forever."

I've had hundreds of meals in five-star restaurants all over the world, but I will always remember the places where I ate with family or friends, for example, watching Nicole devour a Mediterranean lobster at the Hotel Arts Barcelona; eating venison and white asparagus at the InterContinental Hotel in Cologne with Tom Savoy; enjoying salty fish in Istanbul with Caner; eating freshly caught octopus in Göcek, which had been tenderized by Nicole smashing it against the rocks a hundred times; having spaghetti puttanesca at D'Antica in Amsterdam with Jeff and Lee; being served king prawns at the Oriental in Bangkok with George; and eating foie gras at the Hotel Le Negresco in Nice with Paul. I could go on for pages. I find it funny that Kathy gets annoyed when I do not remember to take out the garbage, but I can remember these special meals from thirty years ago. Share a meal and enjoy a drink together with people, and I assure you that it will help connect you with them.

But the best way to connect with others is to do something for someone that they can't do for themselves. In July 2009, while I was riding my Harley on a sunny California afternoon with Nicole on the back, a car cut in front of us, and within seconds we found ourselves scraping against Highway 9. It wasn't pretty. Two medical helicopter rides later, Nicole and I were lying in the ICU of Stanford Hospital. I needed surgery to reattach my left shoulder's humerus bone, and Nicole was all scraped up with a broken leg. The accident happened on a Saturday in the late afternoon, and it was not until Tuesday morning that I was scheduled for surgery. In the interim, I was heavily sedated with painkillers.

After the surgery, as I started feeling human again, my friend Dave came to visit me in the hospital. He was always a joker was trying to cheer me up, but I was still groggy and not in a joking mood. When the nurse brought my lunch, I was not hungry and pushed it away. Dave said, "You have to eat." He spoon-fed me my lunch until it was all gone. Later he also visited Nicole and took her for ice cream in her wheelchair. When we finally returned home, Dave even came by one evening to cook dinner for the family to lighten the load on Kathy. It is a bond that Dave, I, and my family share, and his being there for us during our trying time caused our friendship to become a lot closer. It is a connection that we will always share.

If I were to meet you for the first time, what would be my impression?

- *Do you inform, communicate, or connect with others?*

- *Do you listen to others first and care about their concerns?*

- *Do you look for what you have in common with others or focus on differences?*

- *Do you simplify or complicated things?*

- *Do you inspire others or tear them down?*

8

FAITH AND BIBLICAL PRINCIPLES

Since 1995, my faith has guided my life. It has been my moral compass at the center of all my major decisions. It is part of who I am, so to ignore this topic would be not to provide a complete picture of myself and all the stories in *C Suite and Beyond*. Now if you are not a person of faith, I understand, but I would still encourage you to read on. I think you will find wisdom and some tools that you can apply to your life and your business.

If you are an entrepreneur, the New Testament is one of the best examples of how to build a start-up company and a brand. I am sure you have heard there are riches in niches. Many companies are engaged in competitive warfare, fighting over a few share points in a saturated market, but successful, disruptive companies create new niche markets through innovation. Whenever a company innovates to form a new niche market, over time it always benefits in high profits. In fact, most large markets at one time started as a new idea and a niche market. Cars were a niche market in the horse and buggy days, and Tesla's electric car became the disruptor in the global fossil fuel car industry. Red Bull was the first energy drink, creating a niche market in the saturated beverage industry, followed by a long list of specialty health drinks creating their own niche segments. Facebook, Instagram, and LinkedIn reworked the definition of a friend and reinvented how we share information and how we advertise.

If we go back a bit more than two thousand years, we can use Jesus as a great example of a start-up creating a niche market that eventually turned into a global movement. Jesus created the niche market of Christianity. Hellenism was the mainstream religion of Greece; Romans were animistic; and of course the prevailing religion in the Middle East at the time was Judaism. In a sense, Jesus was an entrepreneur establishing a new product in the form of a new religion. Claiming he was the Son of God, he differentiated himself from all other religions. He eventually became the ultimate sacrifice, the Lamb of God, eliminating the need for all animal sacrifices that once were required to cleanse a person of their sins. Jesus became both the conduit to absolve all sin and the gateway to eternal life.

Many thought he was crazy, and the religious establishment said he was blasphemous, but no one could argue that the product of Christianity was a new concept, highly unique and well-defined. I am not debating a faith or belief system; I am simply stating the main ideas and key differentiators of the one product called

Christianity, which was a new idea, very different from all other religions at the time. To be a market disruptor, one must have an idea that is new, revolutionary, unique, well-defined, and easily understood, one that promises to solve a problem.

As we follow Jesus throughout scripture, we recognize in him the same four keys of leadership success I have been discussing in *C Suite and Beyond*. Jesus created a unique culture among his followers and established a "love at all costs" culture. He also created a clear and simple vision, namely that he was the Son of God and a conduit to the Creator. The growth strategy for Christianity was launched with the great commission through the Holy Spirit, and Jesus built a diverse and balanced team. Let us turn our attention to a brief overview of the four keys and how Jesus put them into action.

Let's start with the fourth key, building a team. Once an idea is born, the start-up company will have to build a team. Many may have difficulty competing for talent in the conventional labor pool. Jesus had the same challenge, so he handpicked a small start-up team of twelve men using unconventional means. He did not recruit established experts from an existing industry; instead he opted for a team with a zest for achievement. He selected the commonest of the common from rural areas, including farmers, a fisherman, a tax collector, and even a political activist. He chose individuals with different strengths to complement each other, picking men with fierce loyalties, amazing passion, courage, and zeal to build a loyal diverse team.

Christ purposely passed over the elite, aristocratic, and influential men of society and chose mostly the men from among the dregs of society. All the religious experts were Jews, yet Jesus did not recruit even one "industry" expert. Instead he chose raw but dedicated people, whom he mentored, trained, and taught. Great leaders understand the importance of a passionate, loyal team and the importance of mentoring their team, which requires an investment of their time. Managers opt for handing off their people for training and do not see the importance of investing their own time into mentoring individuals.

Jesus spent each day walking with his apostles, teaching them through simple parables, and showing them how to perform miracles. He did not send them off to a training course in *miracles 101*. He invested a lot of one-on-one time in mentoring them. Eventually, when he sensed the apostles were ready, he empowered them and delegated to them so they could be his disciples and perform miracles on his behalf. Everyone will benefit from a combination of both training and mentoring; the twelve disciples are a great example how to get a team ready and then empower them for success.

Let's talk about culture, the first key. As the start-up team is being built, the importance of establishing a unique culture is essential. Jesus established a unique culture early on, teaching servant leadership at all costs, and reinforced the values of loving, healing, and teaching through nonviolent actions. In Matthew 22:37 Jesus said, "Love the Lord your God with all your heart and with all your soul and with all your mind," and in verse 39 he said, "Love your neighbor as yourself." Jesus established a "love at all costs" culture, love for God and for each other. There are countless examples in the New Testament underlining Jesus's actions that show his unconditional love for others. For example, in Luke 6:32–36, Jesus reinforces his love culture, instructing us to love our enemies, not just those whom we like. Jesus even rebuked Peter when Peter cut off the high priest servant's ear as they were taking Jesus prisoner. And Jesus prayed for forgiveness for the people who crucified him. It was a unique culture in the Roman Empire era, one filled with greed, self-interest, and violence. Jesus preached a culture of nonviolence, unconditional love, and servant leadership.

In terms of the second key, Jesus also created a clear and simple vision. In Luke 12:8 he said, "I tell you, whoever publicly acknowledges me before others, the Son of Man will also acknowledge before the angels of God. But whoever disowns me before others will be disowned before the angels of God." This is a clear vision showing Jesus as the Son of God and a conduit to the Creator. Vision is long term and should not change. The vision of Christianity is the same today as it was two thousand years ago. In Mark 9:35 Jesus said, "Anyone who wants to be first must be the very last, and the servant of all." Jesus walked the talk to ensure the culture he wished to implement was lived each day. And he led by example, not only by words. Just keep in mind, though, that as much as we would like to live in an ideal world where our team buys into our vision, values, and culture, all companies will experience some dissention like Jesus did with Judas. If you can help it, be proactive and cut the dissenters loose before they come back to bury you.

How about key #3, the growth strategy? Start-ups can make all the grandiose plans they want, but nothing happens until the first product is sold. Jesus's initial focus was on sales, then marketing and eventually operations. You can almost say Jesus was one of the first door-to-door salesmen. At first he took every opportunity to engage individuals or small groups in "direct sales" through his teaching with parables. Jesus also did lot of product demos, performing miracles like healing the sick, raising the dead, turning water into wine, calming the waters, and even walking on water, all to demonstrate his superior product.

Today we recognize that these methods are similar to gorilla marketing. In some ways, with the power of Instagram, Facebook, and LinkedIn, it is easy to replicate these same principles today. It wasn't until Jesus was already a public figure that he added mass media to the marketing mix. His Sermon on the Mount and feeding the crowd of five thousand with five loaves of bread and two fishes was probably his first mass-marketing effort.

Operations should be the last thing a start-up emphasizes, after sales and marketing are well on their way. Jesus implemented operations only after he had established the infrastructure with his disciples and empowered them to set out on the great commission. The great commission was similar to what we know today as manufacturing and distribution of products. The apostles started the distribution of Christianity. Modern-day marketing measures like weighted distribution, reach, and frequency were defined by the disciples as they were starting new churches, engaging them and visiting them frequently, and reinforcing their message.

One last thought on how to attract investment for your start-up. Start-ups tend to go through a very similar evolution process with angel investors, usually family and friends, before moving onto venture capital and eventually public listing. Jesus's early support was also through "angel investors"—family and friends to help build momentum—before he gained wider support from the masses.

This is just one small example of how the Bible is the best resource on how to lead a successful company. In fact, I contend that if we take two companies competing in the same industry with similar products, the one that is led by Christian principles will always be much more successful in the long run. Successful companies in many cases have adopted Christian values and principles; they just don't call it that. If you are an entrepreneur starting a company, remember to start small. Make sure you have a unique concept, focus first on sales, recruit a loyal, well-balanced team, and build momentum as you grow.

In chapter 3, I spoke about the three circles related to having a strong identity: knowing who you are, knowing what your passion is, and knowing what you are good at. I would add one more element and put Christ at the center of the three circles. Faith becomes the glue that holds those three circles together. I call it Christ-centered living, and I will share with you my three circles that are Christianity based. I am a servant leader, I am passionate about adding value to make others better individuals, and I am good at mentoring and empowering people. Without Christ, none of this would be possible. My faith defines me, my passion comes through my faith, and my mentoring gifts are ordained.

In chapter 3, I also spoke about the importance of values and how we learn them at an early age. Values are the foundation of our character. I also said that it is very difficult to learn and adopt values later in life when we become adults. I truly believe this, with one exception. You can adopt a new set of values as an adult if you become born again and start a new life. See, once you accept Christ as your Savior, it requires that you have a paradigm shift and adopt a new set of values and principles to guide your life as a new person. I know when I accepted Christ in my life as an adult in 1996, I made a paradigm shift. I moved from being self-centered to being Christ-centered, and this transformation required that I adopt some new values. Honesty, hard work, and integrity were always part of my value set, but now I added love, respect, humbleness, surrender, and acceptance.

Once I became born again, my life also became much simpler. It has been an ongoing up-and-down journey of learning and improving, but with each step it becomes easier. I have always been blessed with exceptional people skills and found it easy to make connections with most people. Once I rose on the corporate ladder, I was able to leverage this skill to my benefit, but it was always for personal gain. I think the word *manipulation* would be an overstatement, but let's just say Stephen Covey's win-win rule only applied to me if I came out 70 percent ahead and the other person came out 30 percent ahead.

Once I learned how to be a servant leader, I came to understand that the easiest way to achieve success was to make others around me successful. My success is a function of my customers', suppliers', employees', and shareholders' success. I always seek the Holy Spirit's guidance in processes, meetings, and negotiations, and in all other matters. It is amazing how much insight and wisdom we gain if we just learn to listen.

I recall one planning meeting where I was absorbing the information being presented but was not really sure where it was going. I quietly asked the Holy Spirit for guidance and direction. I eventually took over the helm of the meeting with ideas and concepts freely flowing through my words. I attribute this only to what the Holy Spirit had fed me on the spot. I also recall one meeting with a large customer where, in the midst of negotiations, I paused for about twenty seconds, saying a small internal prayer asking the Holy Spirit for guidance. With on-the-spot guidance, I was able to close a very successful deal for our company.

Each day I offer up all my mistakes and victories to our Savior, starting in the morning, when I ask for guidance with the day's agenda, and ending each day with thanks and asking for insight into what I could have done better. I encourage you to seek the Lord's guidance and surround yourself with like-minded believers who will be there to help you with their support and counsel.

Actions have consequences, either good or bad. I met my good friend Dave on a brisk February morning. We had decided to ride our Harleys to Alice's Restaurant. We have been close friends since that time, and both of us have influenced each other. I have been blessed to ride my Harley with all kinds of people, like members of the Hells Angels and members of the motorcycle division of the San Francisco Police Department. When Dave organized the rides we were taking, the groups were mostly comprised of rambunctious guys, and when I organized the rides, they were balanced with more conservative riders. I helped start a motorcycle group called the Sons of Thunder, and we organized rides to spread Christ's fellowship with others. We would always join in a circle and pray before starting the ride, and when stopping for lunch we again prayed before sharing a meal.

On one beautiful Saturday afternoon we had over fifty guys join us riding through the back roads of Sonoma, California, stopping for lunch in Occidental. As the food was being served, we all gathered around to pray. The look on people's faces in the restaurant was priceless. They just could not reconcile in their minds how fifty leather-wearing, scruffy-bearded Harley riders were praying together. The formula was always the same: ride the back-country roads, stop for lunch, and pray before we eat. Over the years, I met many new friends riding my Harley, and I was treated to some amazing hidden gems that most people have never heard of, like feasting on oysters in Marshall General Store, camping in the redwoods, discovering wine country, or exploring small towns like Idyllwild.

About a year after I met Dave, he and Linda joined Kathy and me for dinner one evening. As we were enjoying some fine sushi together, Linda turned to me and said, "I just want to thank you. Dave has changed a lot since you two became friends." I had never tried to preach to Dave or convert him, but I was honest and open about my relationship with the Lord. So many Christians try to disciple through words, but I find it a lot more effective to just have people watch my actions. Unfortunately, too many Christians' words do not match their actions. What you do will influence others and may even bring them to Jesus. Disciple through actions, not just words.

> When a man becomes a Christian, he becomes industrious, trustworthy and prosperous. Now, if that man when he gets all he can and saves all he can, does not give all he can, I have more hope for Judas Iscariot than for that man!
> —*John Wesley*

Stewardship. What does that mean? For me the light first went on when I started giving back. I learned how to give of my time, my knowledge, and my money. Tithing is a cornerstone of Judaism and Christianity. We offer the first 10 percent of our earnings to God, so he may bless the other 90 percent and make it multiply. For many years, I was very frugal with my tithing. I tried to rationalize my giving by pointing to gross margin, operating profit, or whatever else I could justify. I would also factor in the worth of the time I had volunteered at church functions. One day my friend Joe challenged me. "What if you just tithe on net sales?" That was a tough nut to crack, but that was when the light fully went on. Once I stepped up and began to faithfully tithe, my business was blessed beyond imagining. Without faith, it made no sense why this had happened.

It was the same business, the same business model, and the same people, yet our sales had multiplied—for one reason only.

One last thought on faith. Even if you are not a believer, I would encourage you to at least read the book of Proverbs and the book of Ecclesiastes. This short reading will fuel thought-provoking ideas on an endless number of leadership principles. Please read some of the examples I have picked out for you. Let them sink in, then realize the payoffs. There is a world of difference between information, knowledge, and wisdom. Proverbs will yield much wisdom to the open-minded reader. Here are some gems to inspire thought:

- Proverbs 16:23: "The hearts of the wise make their mouths prudent, and their lips promote instruction."

- Proverbs 9:8: "Do not rebuke mockers or they will hate you; rebuke the wise and they will love you. Instruct the wise and they will be wiser still; teach the righteous and they will add to their learning."

- Proverbs 18:2: "Fools find no pleasure in understanding but delight in airing their own opinions."

- Proverbs 10:8: "The wise in heart accept commands, but a chattering fool comes to ruin. Whoever walks in integrity walks securely, but whoever takes crooked paths will be found out."

▸ Proverbs 16:3: "Commit to the Lord whatever you do, and he will establish your plans."

Reading Ecclesiastes is similar to reading a book on the meaning of life, yet it also offers some sound practical advice. For example, *integrity* is a buzzword you hear in business today, but today's meaning is clouded and has been watered down. You'll find that Ecclesiastes 5:5–6 has an absolute definition of integrity: "It is better not to make a vow than to make one and not fulfill it. Do not let your mouth lead you into sin. And do not protest to the temple messenger, 'My vow was a mistake.'"

Or how about the materialistic lifestyles of many people in developed countries? One could argue that Ecclesiastes 5:10–11 serves an early definition of capitalism and consumer marketing. "Whoever loves money never has enough; whoever loves wealth is never satisfied with their income. This too is meaningless. As goods increase, so do those who consume them. And what benefit are they to the owners except to feast their eyes on them?"

Want to know who defined teamwork? Ecclesiastes 4:9–10 is pretty clear about the pitfalls of trying to achieve everything by yourself. "Two are better than one, because they have a good return for their labor: If either of them falls, one can help the other up. But pity anyone who falls and has no one to help them up."

Most of us talk about leaving a legacy, a footprint that shows we made a difference in this world. Ecclesiastes 3:22 nails that thought: "So I saw that there is nothing better for a person than to enjoy their

work, because that is their lot. For who can bring them to see what
will happen after them?"

If you invest time in reading the entire Bible, I promise you will
learn many winning business principles. One quick example is
about empowerment and delegation. Exodus 18:17–26 reads as
follows:

> Moses' father-in-law replied, "What you are doing
> is not good. You and these people who come to
> you will only wear yourselves out. The work is too
> heavy for you; you cannot handle it alone. Listen
> now to me and I will give you some advice, and
> may God be with you. You must be the people's
> representative before God and bring their disputes
> to him. Teach them his decrees and instructions,
> and show them the way they are to live and how
> they are to behave. But select capable men from
> all the people—men who fear God, trustworthy
> men who hate dishonest gain—and appoint them
> as officials over thousands, hundreds, fifties and
> tens. Have them serve as judges for the people at all
> times, but have them bring every difficult case to
> you; the simple cases they can decide themselves.
> That will make your load lighter, because they
> will share it with you. If you do this and God so
> commands, you will be able to stand the strain,
> and all these people will go home satisfied." Moses
> listened to his father-in-law and did everything
> he said. He chose capable men from all Israel and
> made them leaders of the people, officials over

thousands, hundreds, fifties and tens. They served as judges for the people at all times. The difficult cases they brought to Moses, but the simple ones they decided themselves.

Just a few key points. First notice the suggested hierarchy of "thousands, hundreds, fifties and tens." Ten is a good number of direct reports. Take any Fortune 500 organization and the CEO will have on average ten direct reports. C suites usually consist of a matrix structure with core competence positions such as CFO, CIO, CMO, CTO, and COO combined with geographic business units, for example, North America, Latin America, Europe, the Far East, and/or Africa. When the structure gets too big, the COO usually takes on more responsibility, having the CMO and/or CIO et al. report to him or her. A leader needs time to discuss issues with direct reports, so if the number grows much beyond ten, there is just not enough quality time with direct reports. With too many direct reports, people become supervisors or managers, not leaders.

Also notice the comment in Exodus 18:21 about selecting "capable men, men who fear God, trustworthy men who hate dishonest gain." In other words, only hire quality people to build your team and only people who share the company vision, values, and culture. Additionally, notice the instruction in Exodus 18:20: "Teach them his decrees and instructions, and show them the way they are to live and how they are to behave." Once the team is together, make sure there is plenty of mentoring and training to equip each member to succeed. Finally, it become time to empower and delegate to the team when they are ready. Exodus 18:22 instructs us, "Have them serve as judges for the people at all times. The difficult cases they brought to Moses, but the simple ones they decided themselves."

So that in a nutshell is Leadership 101, how to put a winning team together, written about thirty-four hundred years ago.

Good leaders have the ability to remain calm during a crisis. A competitive action, a sudden turn of the market, and a lawsuit can all create chaos and turn a leadership team into a ball of frenzy. As a leader I experienced this several times, but I always had the gift of remaining calm. My CFO Romana asked me one time, "How can you remain so calm in the midst of this crisis?" A team will appreciate and gain confidence from a leader who can remain calm and reassure them that things will be okay. Uncontrolled reactions do not help solve problems. I choose to channel my energy into solutions, not into chaos and panic. My first step is always to ask the Holy Spirit for guidance, then I listen for direction. Matthew 8:24–26 reads, "Suddenly a furious storm came up on the lake, so that the waves swept over the boat. But Jesus was sleeping. The disciples went and woke him, saying, 'Lord, save us! We're going to drown!' He replied, 'You of little faith, why are you so afraid?' Then he got up and rebuked the winds and the waves, and it was completely calm." In the midst of chaos, remain calm and have faith, and the Lord will lead you through it.

In chapter 5, I mentioned that part of any good strategy is knowing how to pivot. My faith has a way of helping me embrace, and change my view of, whatever is happening in my life at any given moment. Napoleon Hill said that every adversity, every failure, every heartache, carries within it the seed of an equal or greater benefit. So whatever life throws at you, whatever business challenge you may have, know this: when you get through it all, you will come out better on the other side. Talking about adversity and a crisis of historic proportions, it does not get any worse than the Crucifixion. But the seed of equal or greater benefit was the resurrection. It does not get any clearer than this.

If you are a person of faith, let scriptures and your faith define you. Live your life by your faith regardless of the circumstance. If you are not a person of faith, read the Good Book as a user manual for humankind, and you will find you'll be more successful practicing these principles.

- ▸ *How much time do you spend reading scripture?*

- ▸ *Are your decisions based on scripture?*

- ▸ *Do you regularly pray and communicate with God?*

- ▸ *Are you listening to the Holy Spirit or just constantly asking for things?*

- ▸ *Do you seek divine guidance on business and personal matters?*

CLOSING

I hope you enjoyed and were entertained by my lifetime collection of stories. I also hope you gained some wisdom along the way. More than that, if I inspired you to become a better leader, then *C Suite and Beyond* has been a blessing to both of us. If there is one point I would like to emphasize, it is that you cannot be a successful leader without developing relationships and having fun with others.

Mother Teresa was one of the most inspiring and humble leaders in my lifetime. Her outlook on life continues to encourage me. One of my favorites is how she views life as an adventure. I love the scene from the movie *The Hurt Locker* where Jeremy Renner, as Staff Sergeant William James, is on home leave and is walking through the supermarket choosing from among hundreds of cereal boxes. You can tell how much he dislikes mundane life versus the excitement of defusing IUDs on the battlefield. What a clear contrast. Some people live to old age yet never really live, spending their lives without achieving anything, just like picking cereal boxes. Others die young but live a life full of love and adventure. I am blessed to be living a life of meaning with a lot of fun along the way.

While living in Budapest in the early 1990s, Kathy and I met and became friends with many other expatriates from all over the world. Unfortunately it was a corporate turnstile with people coming and going each year as their assignments came to an end. Each time a family would leave, Kathy and the other spouses would give them a framed collage of pictures from the times we'd spent together during our stay. Whenever I looked at these collages, I marveled at how many friends we had made and how much fun we had shared in just a short period.

Simon Sinek said, "Life is beautiful not because of the things we see or do. Life is beautiful because of the people we meet." When I reflect on my life, regardless of business, friends, or family, I see that it is one filled with memories and stories of the time I've spent with people. As many successes as I've had in business, they have always been tied to the relationships I had built with my team, customers, or suppliers. Today as I coach executives or lead company workshops, my first criterion is to get to know the people. Only after we form a mini relationship will I accept an assignment. If I do not know the people's underlying challenges and what makes them tick, then how can I possibly help them? The recollections I have with my closest friend Shane, who passed away several years ago, are of us enjoying life together, like celebrating World Series wins at Yankee Stadium, freezing in the Meadowlands watching the New York Giants, sitting in the rain at the US Open, having lunch at Harrods Food Hall, and taking vacations to Prague, Budapest, London, Amsterdam, and Turkey. It would have been meaningless if I had attended alone the live concerts I've seen, including the Beach Boys, the Rolling Stones, Luciano Pavarotti, José Carreras, Andrea Bocelli, and Rod Stewart, among many others, but with Kathy dancing next to me, those concerts are the memories of a lifetime. I once heard it quoted that no one lying on their deathbed wishes they had worked more, but instead wishes they had spent more time with their loved ones. I am not sure I agree 100 percent. Nothing is preventing us from having friends and loved ones whom we work with. If we build close relationships at our workplace and in our businesses, it can be a gratifying and a lot of fun. Work hard, play hard, and learn from your mistakes, and by using my four keys of leadership as your foundation, you will be successful in life. If you can incorporate your faith into the four keys, it will be a slam dunk.

RECOMMENDED READING

In addition to the people whom I mention in *C Suite and Beyond*, including how they touched my life, there are others who influenced me indirectly through their writing. I would recommend the following authors and their books on leadership:

STEPHEN COVEY

The 7 Habits of Highly Effective People

Principle-Centered Leadership

RUDI GIULIANI

Leadership

Time

JOHN MAXWELL

The 15 Invaluable Laws of Growth

The 21 Irrefutable Laws of Leadership

Everyone Communicates, Few Connect

Today Matters

MILES MCPHERSON

The Third option

RONALD REAGAN

The Notes

SIMON SINEK

Find Your Why

The Infinite Game

JACK WELCH

Straight from the Gut

Winning

T om is an industry influencer and is a highly sought-after coach, speaker, educator, and mentor. His approach to leadership comes from a lifetime of international experience. He has built and led executive teams in Fortune 500 companies in Europe, Asia, the Middle East, Latin America, and the United States. His accomplishments include establishing global alliances, acquiring companies, leading successful start-ups, and creating brands.

Tom is a certified member of the John Maxwell group, a leadership training organization built to grow and equip others to do remarkable things and lead fulfilling lives. Tom's servant leadership principles are time proven and founded on biblical principles. "Man of God, leader of men." That vision statement has guided every life choice Tom has made since 1995.

Tom is down to earth and able to strike a balance between business challenges and common-sense solutions. His motivational and engaging style will leave you with practical and applicable solutions that you can put into practice. He is passionate about mentoring and coaching executives. He will empower you, your team, and your company to succeed. Tom is also an international speaker.

CPSIA information can be obtained
at www.ICGtesting.com
Printed in the USA
FSHW011349111120
75642FS